30 Day Whole Food Slow Cooker Challenge

Chef Approved 30 Day Whole Food Slow Cooker Challenge Recipes Made For Your Slow Cooker – Cook More Eat Better

Table of Contents

Introduction

Never before in history have we been so on the move as we are now. Between work schedules, there are a number of other factors to juggle during any given day. It is not at all surprising at the end of a long day, we opt to zip through a fast food restaurant before heading to a kid's soccer game.

The 30 Day Whole Food Slow Cooker Challenge uses Whole30 recipes that can be prepared in a slow cooker. It is designed to optimize your health and fit your busy lifestyle. To skip falling into the fast food trap requires more than thinking ahead. Having dinner Ingredients on standby, waiting for you to arrive home, open the refrigerator and cook is not always enough incentive to bypass a hot meal from a paper bag that can be devoured on the car ride home is available on every corner.

Using a Slow Cooker eliminates the fast food alternatives. You arrive home, you open your cooker and dish out a tasty, hot, nutritious meal. This is where the Whole30 Food Diet comes in. The array of different meals one can make using a slow cooker are not in short supply. The 30 Day Whole Food Slow Cooker Diet is a springboard crafted to launch you in the best direction possible for top-notch health benefits.

The contents of this book will assist you with that in any number of ways. The book's purpose is to arm you with information and inspiration about the Whole30 Food Diet. This includes not only defining Whole30 Foods but providing you with a list of foods that fall into the Whole Food category and of course a number of invigorating Slow Whole30 food recipes that are inspired from a vast selection of seafood, meat, soup, salad, fruit smoothie and dessert plans.

Without getting overly scientific -- this book will discuss how applying the Whole30 Food Diet to your lifestyle will affect your body. In concert with this, we will give you tips on how to use your Slow Cooker, which is going to be incredibly useful, for instance, you will need to know that fish and meat require slightly different Method: than they would on a stove top or oven.

From saving money to saving time...we will go over the practical benefits of a using slow cooker. For now, let's start with a basic question: What are Whole Foods?

Chapter 1: What Are Whole Foods?

Not that that long ago lived a generation of folks for whom meals were the result of what came from the garden. Depending on the season, those foods would have consisted of anything from tomatoes, onions, cucumbers, zucchini, and so on. During that same era, most poultry and red meat came from a neighboring farm and the fish from a nearby stream, sea or lake. All of these foods have one thing in common. They are what we now label as *Whole Food*.

Why is this? Because Whole Foods are foods that are consumable in their natural state. This means they have not been processed or altered with anything artificial. No added color, sugar, or chemicals. When we talk about Whole Foods we are talking about a diet that is made from meat, seafood, veggies, fruits, spices, oils, nuts, and seeds. (You will find a comprehensive list later in the book).

What we are *not* talking about are cereals or anything that comes in a box. No candy bars, no ice cream -- nothing with ingredients you cannot pronounce. If you cannot say it, you probably should think twice before eating it!

By fueling your appetite and your body with easy to make Slow Cooked Whole30 Foods for days, you will be reintroducing yourself to the things your grandparents and great grand parents ate. In this way, the 30 Day Whole Food Slow Cooker

Challenge is about reconnecting. Reconnecting to foods that come from the Earth. Reconnecting to generations from the past. Reconnecting around the dinner table with your family. Reconnecting around the dinner table with your friends.

The ritual of sitting around a dinner table and sharing stories and laughter is alone nourishing. When done together over a plate of steaming warm food, it's heaven. In this way, the Slow Cooker is like a time machine that creates the opportunity to engage in a past time most of us do not otherwise have time for.

Now, let's shift from Whole Foods and Slow Cooking to the topic of the Whole30 Diet. The purpose of this diet is ultimately to rid the body of toxins, enable weight loss, reestablish your relationship with food by replacing unhealthy cravings and habits with healthy ones. This, in turn, will increase your metabolism, aid in promoting normal digestion and balance your immune system, thus your overall health!

It is often described as a diet that "resets" the body.

The benefits of resetting your will have a domino effect. When you begin introducing Whole30 Foods into your daily repertoire you will begin to feel more energetic and more in tune with your life since the sugar coated, artificial intake has ended. Let's look at some basic question and answers.

I have been eating regular foods for all my life and I feel healthy. Why should I consider a Whole30 Food Diet?

Consuming Whole30 Foods means you are eliminating sugars and an array of additives from compromising your body's ability to function organically. This is why the effect of the diet is often referred to as a "reset." You are flushing out things the body does not need and cannot use.

What is so great about an organically functioning body?

There are numerous benefits to your body as chemically free as possible. For example, your liver will not have to work overtime trying to rid pollution from your body. Your body will feel less exhausted without this extra work and you will have more energy. Your hormones will not be compromised by exposure to growth enhancing additives. This will give your mood a lift. Less sugar will result in low blood pressure. Your skin, hair, and nails will strengthen as your body is better able to extract needed nutrients from the food. The list goes on and on...

Overall, the proof is in the pudding--as long as there is no sugar in it!

Conclusion...

The best way to learn about the Whole30 Foods and a Slow Cooking Diet is through first-hand experience.

Chapter 2: What Are The Benefits Of Using A Slow Cooker?

There are several, beginning with they save you time and require less effort than standard cooked meals. Yes, some of the recipes require more prep time than others. It is important to remember, mindfully putting time into preparing food for you and your family can be a very fulfilled experience.

On days when you do not feel pushed for time, consider recipes that require more Method:. Likewise, on busy days, pick meal plans that have minimal steps. In general, soups and stews are often incredibly fast and effortless. You can toss in all the required indredients in without fussing over them much, if at all.

Time saved.

Slow Cookers allow for time flexibility. If you know you have a busy morning, you can get everything for your next day's meal set up the night before. All you have to do is prepare your dinner. Add the indredients to your slow cooker which is designed to withstand the cold. Meaning, you can place it in your refrigerator overnight. You should take it out first thing in the morning to allow the cooker to warm a bit before turning it on (20 mins will do the trick).

Money saved.

Using a slow cooker is money saving for a number of reasons, one of them is that you can buy less expensive but high-quality meats that no one else wants because they take too long to cook. Cuts such as pork and lamb shoulder, beef brisket, roasts, pork chops and goose are an end of the day delight!

Health!

Slow Cookers are a healthy choice. Unlike frying pans, slow cookers do not require you add butter or oil. In fact, it is advisable to trim the fat from your meats as much as possible before adding them to your slow cooker. If you don't, you can end up with an undesired pool of fat in your finished product.

This is because of the nature of the slow cooker. Vegetables, seafood and meats are cooked in steam. As such, they are perpetually being seasoned by a blend of everything that is decorating the pot. I think this is probably an opportune time to mention that your slow cooker comes with a watertight seal.

Chapter 3: What Are Some Tips On How To Best Use My Slow Cooker?

Slow cookers have water tight lids that seal when you close them. The lid is sealed to prevent the liquid from inside the cooker from evaporating. This is important to know in the event that you are adapting a standard recipe to use in your cooker.

In this case, it the standard recommendation is that you should reduce liquids by roughly a third.

Another way to measure this is visually. Liquids should just cover your meat and vegetables.

What happens if there is too much liquid? Nothing that cannot be repaired. The worst case scenario is that your cooker will leak out the top and food inside will not cook properly.

Half to two-thirds full is ideal and certainly no more than three quarters.

No gravy train.

Meats cooked using your slow cooker will steam cook. The broth produced will not thicken. It cannot because that is how it goes with slow cookers verse an oven. They are differently designed and created to do different things. There is nothing to overcome in using a slow cooker apart from recognizing it is a new kitchen tool that, like an over, has certain abilities and attributes that an oven does not.

Slow cooking.

An ability slow cookers feature is they are meant to be on for hours and hours and hour. Something one would not dare do with an oven is leave it "on" and pop over to a neighbor's house for a chat. It may take a while to get used to it. The very best way to render excellent meals is by turning your slow cooker on "low" and leaving the house for several hours.

Slow cookers are made to be left on their own. The cooking process will be offset by a hands-on chef who is constantly opening and closing the lid. The lid should stay firmly shut and not be opened for any reason for the slow cooker to efficiently do its thing. Letting heat out will compromise its abilities. That said in the case that you do open the lid, just increase the cooking time accordingly.

What's easiest to master using a slow-cooker?

One reason soups and stews have a glorious relationship with the slow cooker is that indredients can be added in one fell swoop. Recipes, such as those that call for fish and herbs will require you add these things towards the end. This does not make fish recipes more difficult to make. It just means you there are a few steps to take before dinner will be ready.

15

As with everything, using a slow cooker will take some experimentation. Things, such as onions can be fried up beforehand and then added. Alternatively, they can be added in their raw form. However, depending on what Method: is used, will affect the flavor of the meal. Obviously, the best thing to do is to try recipes both ways and decide which is preferable to your and your family's palate.

To Sear or not to Sear?

The same that is true of onions is true for meats. You can sear meat before adding it to your slow cooker or not. If you are a diehard lover for that caramel browned layer, this cannot be achieved using a slow cooker.

Chicken and Chicken Skins

Like with meats, slow cookers don't do a lot to transform chicken skins into anything remarkable. They surface hot and a bit soggy. The rule of thumb is either sear them up before adding them to your slow cooker or removing and discarding the skins altogether. It's up to you!

Chapter 4: What Is the Whole Foods 30 Day Challenge?

The 30 Day Whole Food Slow Cooker challenge eliminates sugars and additives from your meals. By using a Slow Cooker and preparing meals consisting of meats, seafood, veggies, fruits, spices, oils, nuts, and seeds, your body will wake up to its full potential.

Without sugar and unnatural chemical additives, you will sleep restfully. In turn, you will begin to have more energy. Not just because of increased stints of pleasurable sleep. With only clean foods traveling through your bloodstream, your body will not have to work as hard to clean toxins out that otherwise pass through the liver to be filtered.

Participation requires only a one-month commitment. For our part, we have compiled recipes for you to use. And, we have customized a 30-day meal plan (included in this book) you may choose to use to assist your food shopping and meal planning for the duration of the diet.

Our overarching aim is to give you as much useful information as possible. We think being on a diet is not limited to eating restrictions. Understanding why you are doing this and not doing that is part of the diet. We have done our best to anticipate your needs and fill in the blanks where we can. If we could, we would come to your homes and cook for you!

Because we cannot cook for you, we have included in our book everything from shopping lists to detailed recipes, and a whole lot of hope and encouragement. We are certain you are worth it!

What are Whole30 foods? What aren't?

Whole Foods do not contain artificial additives of any kind. One way to know this is by identifying a food's source. Read your labels. Make the best decision possible. Use the list we have put together for you here to guide your decisions. There are a lot (and I mean A LOT) of blogs out there that offer their version of the Whole30 Food Diet along with an endless array of recipes.

We have consequently done our best to sift through them all and compile a list of dietary information that is most often agreed upon. We have created recipes that are meaningful, creative, diverse, nutritious and compliment the Whole30 Diet with its standard list of things that are off the table. Most everywhere one reads about the diet they will find the restrictions are the following:

THE NO GO ZONE

NO sugar

This means sugar that is real and artificial sugars are off the table. No syrup, honey, agave nectar, coconut sugar, date syrup, stevia, Splenda, Equal, Nutrasweet, xylitol, etc.

No alcohol

This includes alcohol in all forms, even if for cooking. Alcohol is one of those hidden sources of sugar and for the purpose of this diet is off limits.

No grains

What are we talking about? This pertains to wheat, rye, oats, corn, rice, barley, millet, bulgur, sorghum, sprouted grains – including quinoa, amaranth, buckwheat.

No legumes

No beans of all kinds black, red, pinto, navy, white, peas, chickpeas, lentils, and peanuts. You know what that means: no peanut butter! As soy falls into the bean category, it, too off the table -- in all forms. Soy sauce, tempeh, tofu. ***Green beans, sugar snap peas, and snow peas are the exception to this rule.*

No dairy

Yogurt and ice cream are off the menu for a month. As are cow, goat, or sheep's milk products like milk, cream, cheese, kefir, yogurt, sour cream. Products such as Almond Milk are fine.

NO Carrageenan, MSG, and Sulfites

Read your labels. These additives are often found in processed foods and/or sold as "seasoning packs." They are often loaded with sodium and other things you really should not put into your body.

Are you left wondering what you CAN eat? The answer is that there is a lot more on the "Yes" list than the "No" list. This, of course, is the answer behind why the diet varies. It is not entirely possible to create a list of foods that are allowed. This means that overall the Whole30 Diet is ever-evolving.

This also means there is not a need to memorize the list of foods on the "Yes" list. Instead, focus on the "No" list to make decisions about food choices.

THE GREEN ZONE!

Fruits

Apple
Applesauce
Apricots
Avocado
Blackberries
Blueberries
Cantaloupe
Cherries
Dates
Figs
Grapefruit
Grapes
Green Beans
Honeydew melon
Kiwi
Mandarin oranges

Mango
Nectarine
Orange
Papaya
Peach
Pears
Pineapple
Plums
Prunes
Raisins
Raspberries
Strawberries
Snap Peas
Snow Peas
Tangerines
Watermelon

Vegetable

Artichoke
Asparagus
Bean sprouts
Beets
Broccoli
Brussels sprouts
Cabbage

Carrots
Cauliflower
Celery
Cucumber
Eggplant
Green onions or scallions

Greens
Green beans
Kohlrabi
Leeks
Mushrooms
Okra
Onions
Pea Pods
Peppers
Radishes

Salad greens
Sauerkraut
Spinach
Squash
Tomatoes
Turnips
Water chestnuts
Watercress
Zucchini

Meat

Beef
Round Sirloin
Flank Steak
Tenderloin
Roast Steak
Ground beef
(lean)
Corned beef
Short ribs
Prime rib
(trimmed)
Pork

Ham
Canadian bacon
Tenderloin
Center loin chop
Bostonbutt
Poultry
Chicken
Turkey
Cornish Hen
Duck
Goose

Fish & Shellfish

Catfish
Clams
Cod
Crab
Flounder
Haddock
Halibut
Herring

Lobster
Oysters
Trout
Tuna
Salmon
Sardines
Scallops
Shrimp

Coffee & Teas

Brewed Coffee (Can Add Coconut or Almond Milk)
Iced Coffee
Cold Brew Coffee
Americano
Espresso
Herbal Teas (Unsweetened)

Fruit Juices

1/2c to 1c of 100%
Fruit juice with no sugar
Apple juice/cider
Cranberry juice cocktail
Fruit juice blends
Grape juice
Grapefruit juice
Orange juice
Pineapple juice
Prune juice

Red-Light Foods: Stop!

- NO additional bread or cereals
- NO cookies (dry or sweet), cake, or pastry
- NO sugar, syrup, chocolate, sweets, cocoa, honey, jam
- NO alcoholic drinks, sweetened fruit drinks, or sugar-sweetened carbonated beverages

Chapter 5: Whole Food Slow Cooker Challenge Meat Recipes

You can have your cake and eat it, too! Slow cooking Whole30 meat dishes gives you the means to enjoy exceptional and familiar meals while dieting and juggling a fuller than full lifestyle. To help you select meals, we have shared some tips here with you to help enhance the outcome of your dishes.

Sometimes planning a meal is a matter of time and not a matter of appetite. On really busy days when you plan to be gone for several hours these meat recipes are your best go-to option. With a slow cooker, they can take anywhere from 6-9 hours on a low temperature setting. Meat is thick and metabolically tougher than fish.This gives meat a cooking versatility that fish cannot offer which is why it is better to save fish entrees for days when you are at home or will be out for only 1 - 3 hours.

Using a slow cooker with meat dishes can render some gourmet level dishes but it does take time to fine tune the process of using a slow cooker as opposed to an oven or stove top. We have added information about searing meats from the introduction again here to remind you of the reasons why searing adds to the flavor and presentation of a meal.

Along with searing, to make these meat entrees truly spectacular consider mindfully pairing them with sides. This does not always mean a salad. Consider easy to prepare vegetable dishes, such as roasted bell pepper or skewered mushrooms. Just make sure it is on your list of Whole30 indredients!

To Sear or not to Sear?

The same that is true of onions is true for meats. You can sear meat before adding it to your slow cooker or not. If you are a diehard lover for that caramel browned layer, this cannot be achieved using a slow cooker.

Chicken and Chicken Skins

Like with meats, slow cookers don't do a lot to transform chicken skins into anything remarkable. They surface hot and a bit soggy. The rule of thumb is either sear them up before adding them to your slow cooker or removing and discarding the skins altogether. It's up to you!

For the purpose of keeping with the Whole30 diet, some recipes call for *coconut aminos*. If you are like most people, you have not heard of them before. They are rising in popularity as they are being used to replace of soy sauce, which you will be delighted to know tastes almost identical!

Adriatic Marinated Meatballs

Inspired by the tomato growing region in the south the Italy where nutrient rich land kisses the fresh sea water. Adriatic Married Meatballs are an Italian inspired dish that is a zesty filling treat. They are easy to make and tend to appeal even to the pickiest of eaters.

Tomatoes offer a high dose of vitamin C. Partner them with iron rich meatballs and you have the beginning of a beautiful relationship!

Ingredients (meatballs):

- 1 and ¾ lbs ground beef
- 1 egg
- ¼ cup blanched almond flour
- ¾ teaspoon fine grain sea salt, divided
- 2 teaspoon onion powder
- ½ teaspoon garlic powder
- 1 tablespoon Italian seasoning blend
- A pinch crushed red pepper

Ingredients (Sauce):

- 1 - 28 oz can crushed tomatoes with basil
- 1 - 14 oz can diced tomatoes with basil and garlic
- 1 - 6 oz can tomato paste
- ½ medium onion, chopped
- 2 tablespoon chopped fresh garlic
- 2 tablespoon chopped fresh oregano leaves
- 2 bay leaves
- sea salt to taste

Method:

1. Meatballs: In a small bowl, mix together the almond flour, ½ teaspoon of the sea salt, onion and garlic powder, Italian seasoning, and crushed red pepper.

2. In a large bowl, add the ground beef and sprinkle evenly with the remaining sea salt. Add the egg and almond flour mix (plus parsley if adding) and gently mix with your hands until the mixture binds and is evenly distributed.

3. Line a large baking sheet with parchment paper and preheat your broiler.

4. Form the meat mixture into 20 meatballs and arrange on the baking sheet. Broil 2-4 minutes just to lightly brown and release a small amount of fat (this avoids an overly greasy sauce) and remove promptly. This will enhance their flavor .

5. Now, you are ready to add your meatballs to the slow cooker.

6. Top the meatballs with all sauce indredients.

7. Cover. Cook on low for 4 hours, until meatballs are cooked through

8. Let meat set for 2 - 3 minutes before serving.

Lincolnshire Lamb

Despite jokes about British culinary capabilities, some dishes the English can proudly claim ownership over. Lincolnshire Lamb Roast is just one of them. Without a doubt, this recipe drew its inspiration from the undulating hills and gregarious gardens of the Lincolnshire countryside where breathing the air alone increases even the most feeble appetite.

Parsnips pack a punch of vitamin C and are loaded with magnesium. Lamb is high in protein and exploding with B12 along with iron, which is essential for blood production.

Ingredients:

- 4 lb leg of lamb (with the bone for the best flavor)
- A pinch of sea salt and pepper
- 1 tablespoon olive oil
- ½ cup chicken broth*
- 6 cloves garlic, finely chopped
- 2 sprigs rosemary, chopped
- 2 sprigs thyme, stripped off stalk
- ⅓ cup stone ground mustard
- 2 carrots, peeled and chopped
- 2 parsnips, peeled and chopped
- 1 small rutabaga, peeled and chopped
- ½ teaspoon sea salt
- ¼ teaspoon black pepper
- *additive free broth

Method:

1. For the best possible flavor, sear your lamb until it develops a nice golden crust.
2. (To Sear) Dry your lamb very well with paper towel and season with a couple generous pinches of salt and pepper. Heat a cast iron skillet over high heat, add olive oil. You want the pan extremely hot.
3. Sear on both sides, 3 to 4 minutes a side until you get most of the roast seared. Remove the meat from the pan and then reduce the heat to medium, at which point you will add the chicken broth while at the same time scraping up the brown from the bottom of the pan.
4. Put your lamb in the slow cooker.
5. In a small bowl, mix the garlic, rosemary, thyme and mustard. Pour it on top of the lamb and use your hands to coat the meat with the mixture.
6. Toss the chopped root veggies (carrots, parsnips, potato and rutabaga) with salt and pepper, and arrange them around the meat. Pour the chicken broth from when you deglazed the pan on top of the veggies.
7. Cook on low for 8 to 10 hours.
8. Let meat set for 2 - 3 minutes before serving.
9. Serve with a green salad or veggie.

Louisiana Steam

The combination of sweet and spice is similar to a hot summer night. This recipe marries the best of both worlds by coupling delicate mango and zesty chicken with a variety of spices. We are talking about everything from ginger to habanero pepper. The inspiration for this explosive entree emerged from along the bayous of Louisiana, where one can find steam run ships and steamy culinary dishes.

Mango is high in vitamin C and chicken offers up a good amount of protein. The benefits: ginger is packed with an array of medicinal properties and is high in potassium.

Ingredients:

- 1/2 cup orange mango juice (not from concentrate)
- 1/4 cup coconut milk*
- 1 tablespoon fresh ginger minced
- 1-1 1/2 teaspoon habanero pepper minced
- 1/2 tablespoon garlic minced
- 1/2 tablespoon coconut aminos
- 1/4 teaspoon sea salt
- 2 medium sweet potatoes peeled and chopped into large wedges
- 1 lb chicken breasts
- 2 teaspoon curry powder
- 1 1/2 tablespoon unsweetened coconut flakes
- 1 mango cubed
- cilantro for garnish
  To assure it is whole30, use coconut milk with no sulfites

Method:

1. Whisk together 1/2 cup orange mango juice, coconut milk, ginger, garlic, habanero pepper, coconut aminos and salt in your slow cooker. Place the sweet potato wedges in an even layer.
2. Sprinkle both sides of the chicken breast with the curry powder, and a pinch of salt and pepper, and rub evenly.
3. Lay the chicken breast on top of the sweet potatoes, cover, and cook on low heat until the sweet potatoes are soft and the chicken is tender, about 6-7 hours.
4. Using a slotted spoon, gently remove the chicken and sweet potatoes to a large plate.
5. In a separate small bowl, whisk together the remaining 3 teaspoons of juice and until smooth. Whisk into the sauce mixture in the slow cooker.
6. Place the sweet potatoes and chicken back into the slow cooker, cover, and turn the heat up to high. Cook for an additional 1 hour - 1 hour 15 minutes, until the sauce is nice and thick.
7. While the sauce thickens, heat your oven to 350 degrees and spread the coconut flakes onto a small baking sheet. Bake until golden brown, about 2-4 minutes.
8. When the sauce has thickened, divide the chicken and sweet potatoes between 4 bowls.
9. Divide the cubed mango and toasted coconut flakes onto each bowl.
10. Let meat set for 2 - 3 minutes before serving.
11. Garnish with cilantro, serve and enjoy!

KC Short Ribs

You know the rule -- if you are going to eat ribs, make sure the recipe you use of originates from that south! Actually, Kansas is arguably not a southern state which if funny because it is also believed to be the state from where BBQ Ribs were first made. With that, we have put together a recipe that comes about as close to perfect as one can get when using a slow cooker to recreate this all American finger licking dish.

Believe it or not, ribs have a glorious about of protein and are richer than rich source of B12. While it is not advisable to eat them more than once or twice a month, they are worthy of diving into from time to time.

Ingredients:

- 2 pounds short ribs beef*
- 1 tablespoon olive oil
- 4 pieces bacon chopped 1-inch pieces *
- 1 onion cut into quarters and then thinly sliced
- 1 head garlic
- 4 shallots peeled and cut into quarters
- 4 cups chicken broth or beef*
- 2 sprigs thyme large stems removed
- 1 bay leaf
- salt to taste
- pepper to taste

*Beef ribs with bones will render the most flavor, boneless varieties will, however, work too for this recipe

Bacon (be careful to read the label, avoid corn syrup)
buy additive free broth

Method:

1. Season short ribs with salt and pepper. For the most flavor, in a large skillet over medium-high heat, sear the short ribs in the olive oil on all sides until brown. Add to slow cooker.
2. In the same skillet, add the bacon, onion, garlic, and shallots. Cook together and stir until the bacon begins to brown.
3. Transfer all this to your slow cooker.
4. You are ready now to add your broth, bay leaf, and thyme to the slow cooker. After adding the herbs, set the cooker on high for 5 - 6 hours. To test whether or not it is finished, the meat should be falling off the bone.
5. Spoon the bay leaf out with a spoon.
6. Strain the cooking liquid for homemade gravy to pour over top before serving. Season with salt and pepper.
7. Garnish with fresh thyme.
8. Let meat set for 2 - 3 minutes before serving.

Marrakesh Express

This tagine recipe takes chicken to a new level of good. Moroccan spices add a new wave of flavor and a wealth of beneficial health prospects to your kitchen. Turmeric is an excellent source of magnesium. It is also known to act as an anti inflammatory and antioxidant. Likewise, cumin aids with digestion, disease prevention and lowering of blood sugar.

If these spices are not already lining the shelves of your kitchen, they will find themselves welcomes guests as you will learn, they can add a surprise twist to staple foods you want to decorate with a little zing and zazz.

Ingredients:

- 1 tablespoon paprika
- 2 teaspoons ginger
- 2 teaspoons turmeric
- 2 teaspoons cumin
- 2 teaspoons pepper
- 2 teaspoons allspice
- 1 ½ teaspoons salt
- 1 onion peeled and sliced
- 1 whole chicken cut into parts (back and giblets removed)
- 1 ½ pounds sweet potatoes cut into 1-inch pieces
- 1 large tomato cored and cut into wedges
- ½ pound green beans trimmed and cut in half
- 4 large carrots peeled and cut into 1-inch pieces
- 1 cup peas frozen

- 1 large zucchini or 2 small
- ¼ ounce jar green olives or 1 cup
- 3 cloves garlic minced
- ⅓ cup cilantro fresh

Method:

1. In a small bowl mix together the paprika, ginger, turmeric, cumin, pepper and salt with a fork -- set aside.
2. Mix the onion in the bottom of a slow cooker. Add the chicken parts on top. Sprinkle with half the seasoning mix.
3. Add your sweet potatoes, tomato, green beans, carrots, peas, zucchini, green olives, and garlic.
4. Sprinkle with the remaining spice mix and gently toss the veggies together.
5. Top with fresh cilantro, cover your slow cooker and set on high for 4 to 5 hours or until the chicken is tender enough to fall off the bone.
6. Let meat set for 2 - 3 minutes before serving.

You can also cook this on low for 7 to 8 hours.

Moorland Thyme and Chicken

Outside the hustle and bustle of London, England's lush hillsides are ripe farmland. Food served there is simple, yet fulfilling. Moorland thyme and chicken is a classic recipe that adapts easily to a slow cooker without giving up any of what makes the dish a long lasting tradition.

Chicken is rich in protein, lemon in vitamin C. Thyme is loaded with potassium and like other herbs offers many medicinal benefits.

Ingredients:

- 1 whole chicken (3-4 pounds)
- 1/4 cup fresh squeezed lemon juice
- 5 sprigs of fresh thyme
- 2-3 bay leaves
- 3-5 whole cloves of garlic, peeled
- 1 teaspoon sea salt
- 1/4 teaspoon black pepper

Method:

1. Remove giblets from the chicken and rinse under cool water -- place in slow cooker.
2. Pour lemon juice over whole chicken and sprinkle with sea salt, pepper, and thyme.
3. Place garlic cloves and bay leaves in the slow cooker around the chicken.

4. Cover slow cooker and cook the chicken on low for 9-10 hours OR high for 4-5 hours, depending on your schedule.

5. Once the chicken is done cooking, the meat should easily come off the bone and you can enjoy it immediately but...

6. Let meat set for 2 - 3 minutes before serving.

Seven Bridges Road

The long and scenic drive to the most southern reaches of the US is enhanced by the food one eats along the way there. Seven Bridges Road is a culinary marriage between staple southern foods and their counterparts from far away lands. Pork, turmeric, cumin and curry colliding with coconut milk not only offers endless health benefits -- each of these spices is celebrated for their medicinal properties -- they taste incredible when blended together. It is a little like taking your mouth on an exotic vacation!

Pork is rich in B12, B6, Thiamin (B1), Niacin (B3). What happens when you get all those B vitamins together? They convert food into fuel that gives the body a nice energy pick-me-up. Thiamine aids many body functions including the nervous system, muscle function, and helping out electrolytes by enabling them to transport themselves in and out of nerve cells, muscle cells , as well as digestion and carbohydrate metabolism.

Ingredients:

- 2 tablespoons coconut oil
- 4 pounds boneless pork shoulder, cut into 2-inch pieces
- Salt and freshly ground pepper
- 1 large onion, chopped
- 3 garlic cloves, minced
- 3 tablespoons minced fresh ginger
- 1 tablespoon mild curry powder
- 1 tablespoon ground cumin

- ½ teaspoon ground turmeric
- One 14-ounce can diced tomatoes
- 1 cup unsweetened coconut milk*
- 2 cups chicken stock or low-sodium broth

To assure it is whole30, use coconut milk with no sulfites

Method:

1. In a large skillet, heat the coconut oil.
2. Brown pork working in batches, seasoning with salt and pepper -- transfer cooked pork to slow cooker.
3. Leave about 2 tablespoons coconut oil in the skillet and add the onion, garlic, ginger, curry, cumin and turmeric and cook over low heat, stirring, until fragrant and the onion is softened, about 5 minutes -- add mixture to the slow cooker.
4. Finally, add your tomatoes and their juices, coconut milk and stock, cover and cook on high for 4 hours.
5. Let meat set for 2 - 3 minutes before serving.

Remove as much fat from the surface of the stew as possible. Garnished with cilantro and scallions.

San Sebastian Tagine

It may or may not come as a surprise to you, Spain has some of the world's most delicious foods. Even spanish tomatoes are said to be more flavorful and ripe with flavor than tomatoes from anywhere else. The next best thing to having the world's best indredients is having the recipes those indredients inspire.

San Sebastian Tagine is one of those dishes! It is made from a combination of vegetable and chicken that were first mixed on the shore of San Sebastian beaches. The recipe has notable undertones of Moroccan influence that impact the flavor and sense that this meal comes from somewhere far away -- despite this, it is dead easy to make!

Carrots, green peppers and squash all give you a healthy dose of vitamins C and B. The chicken will give you and your loved ones a lot of protein.

Ingredients:

- ½ pound baby carrots
- 1 cup chopped green peppers
- 1 cup chopped onion
- 2 tablespoons lemon juice
- 1 teaspoon ginger
- 1 medium butternut squash, cut into 2 inch cubes
- 1 can chickpeas, drained
- 2 cans diced tomatoes
- 1 ½ pounds boneless, skinless chicken thighs or chicken breast
- 3 tablespoons allspice

Method:

1. In a 5-6 quart slow cooker, combine carrots, peppers, onion, lemon juice, ginger, squash, chickpeas, and tomatoes.
   Sprinkle with 2 tablespoons allspice -- mix together.
2. Lay chicken thighs on top of veggies.
3. Sprinkle with remaining seasoning.
4. Cover and cook on low for 8 hours -- salt and pepper to taste.
5. Remove chicken and shred. Stir back into stew. Or serve thighs whole on top of veggies in a soup bowl.
6. Let meat set for 2 - 3 minutes before serving.

Syracuse Chicken and Olives

From the southern reaches of Italy's shores is the island of Sicily is the city of Syracuse. It was once a Greek dominated city that sported a thriving arts scene along with a great many recipes influenced by both the sea and the rich olive growing region. It is not surprising, some of these culinary dishes have lingered over the centuries, changeling only slightly.

Syracuse Chicken and Olives will take your breath away! It is rich with tomatoes and earthy herbs and is very straight forward in terms of Method:.

The chicken is rich in protein, tomatoes in vitamin C and olives in flavor!

Ingredients:

- 2 pounds boneless, skinless chicken breasts
- 1 can diced tomatoes
- 1 can tomato sauce
- 1 onion thinly sliced
- 4- 6 garlic cloves, whole
- ½ cup balsamic vinegar
- 2 tablespoons virgin olive oil
- 12 pitted kalamata olives
- palmful herb mix: thyme, basil, rosemary, oregano
- ground black pepper
- salt to taste

41

Method:

1. Pour the olive oil into the bottom of the slow cooker.
2. Place the chicken breasts into the slow cooker. Season with salt and pepper.
3. Top each breast with sliced onion, garlic cloves and Italian herbs.
4. Pour in vinegar, tomatoes and tomato sauce.
5. Cook on high about 4 hours.
6. Remove chicken breasts, slice as desired and place back in the tomato/vinegar sauce.
   Add olives and let them warm through for about ten minutes.
7. Let meat set for 2 - 3 minutes before serving.

Bombay Curry Chicken

Obviously, when gathering recipes for the Whole30 diet we wanted to eliminate the idea of food restrictions by finding compelling and enticing recipes to enhance your day to day experience. Bombay Curry Chicken not only takes us around the world, it takes a step back in time.

This colonially inspired recipe contains gestures from both the British Empire and India. With both these remarkable countries flavoring the outcome, one cannot go wrong. The recipe is a compilation of spices all of which are medicinally beneficial. The chicken is full of vitamins, minerals and protein. Sweet potatoes are immensely rich in vitamin A which helps protect a number of body organs, the immune system, and one's vision. Get cooking and see for yourself!

Ingredients:

- 3-4 boneless skinless chicken breasts, cut into bite sized pieces
- 3-4 sweet potatoes chopped into bite sized pieces
- 2 tablespoons white vinegar
- ¼ cup + 2 tablespoons curry powder
- ½ tablespoon salt, or to taste
- 1 teaspoon black pepper, or to taste
- 1 cup chopped peppers
- 3 green chile peppers, sliced lengthwise but not in two
- 6-8 green cardamom pods
- 6 whole cloves
- 10 curry leaves
- 1 cinnamon stick

- 1 teaspoon ground ginger
- 3 cloves garlic, minced
- 2 tablespoons tomato paste
- 1 cup water or chicken broth
- 1/2 cup coconut milk*

**To assure it is whole30, use coconut milk with no sulfites*
**Chicken broth without additives*

Method:

1. Cut the chicken into bite sized pieces. Combine the vinegar, 1/4 cup curry powder, salt, and pepper in the slow cooker. Toss to coat the chicken.
2. Add chopped onions, sliced chile peppers, cardamom pods, cloves, curry leaves, cinnamon stick, ginger, garlic, and tomato paste to chicken mixture.
3. Cut sweet potatoes into bite size pieces then coat with remainder 2 tablespoons of curry powder.
4. Place sweet potatoes in slow cooker .
5. Add water or chicken broth to slow cooker .
6. Cook on high 2 hours then low 3-4 more hours or until sweet potatoes are soft and chicken is done.
7. Add coconut milk and cook for 20-30 more minutes.
8. Let meat set for 2 - 3 minutes before serving.

Pepperdine Steak

For decades California has been referred to as "The Garden of Eden" for good reason. There is almost nothing that does not grow there. Complimenting their rich agriculture is beef. The Pepperdine Steak was introduced around the time of the Gold Rush. When adventurers made their way across the country were lucky enough to strike gold, it was customary to tell others they were on the way to "get peppered" as they made their way down the Sierra Nevada hills toward San Francisco. That is where gold was traded for cash and cash could buy a Pepperdine Steak.

The Pepperdine is easy to make. On those days when you feel particularly hungry, this is an excellent choice. It is traditional and satisfying in every way. Your body will think so, too. Pepperdine Steak is rich in B vitamins and minerals. Add to that the bell peppers offer up some vitamin C, A and B6.

Ingredients:

- 1 pound beef steak, lean
- ¾ cup bell pepper, green, strips
- 1/2 cup bell pepper, red, strips
- 1/2 cup bell pepper, yellow, strips
- 1/2 cup onion, sliced
- 1 clove garlic
- 6 teaspoons coconut aminos1 teaspoon black pepper

Method:

1. Cut round steak, peppers and onions into strips, removing as much fat as possible from steak.
2. Sear steak in pan over med. high heat.
3. Press clove of garlic into crock, add all indredients.
4. Cover. Cook on Low for 8-10 hours.
5. Let meat set for 2 - 3 minutes before serving.

Natchez Weekend

Natchez is not the popular destination that New Orleans is. Nonetheless, this historic town draws a lot of attention. Apart from its rich history and its architecture, its food is a thing to behold and marvel. Natchez Weekend was cultivated out of need. When friend and family decide on a whim they were heading to visit Natchez for the weekend, those on the receiving end needed dish that could be whipped together in a flash that appeared and tasted as if it had been labored over for hours in the kitchen. Apart from this time it takes to go to the store, Natchez Weekend requires 6 hours to cook and about 10 minutes to prep.

Pork is rich in B12, B6, Thiamin (B1), Niacin (B3). What happens when you get all those B vitamins together? They convert food into fuel that gives the body a nice energy pick-me-up. Thiamine aids many body functions including the nervous system, muscle function, and helping out electrolytes by enabling them to transport themselves in and out of nerve cells, muscle cells , as well as digestion and carbohydrate metabolism.

Ingredients:

- 1 smoked pork hock
- 1 jar whole white pearl onions
- 16 ounces ham
- 16 ounces green beans**
- 4 baking sweet potatoes, diced

**If beans are frozen, it is not necessary to thaw them before adding them to the pot!*

Method:

1. Combine all indredients in slow cooker.
2. Cook on low for 6 hours.
3. Let meat set for 2 - 3 minutes before serving.

Wellfleet And Vine

The sandbar that is Cape Cod grows a surprising array of fruits and vegetables. Wellfleet Vine is a lesser known recipe that comes to us from the quiet village of Wellfleet which is located not far from a number of cranberry bogs. Every year when the bogs are ready for that year's cranberries to be harvested, locals begin testing news ways to use cranberries. They are, after all, a prolific fruit!

Pork loin became a favored meat to use alongside the cranberry. It is not surprising. The cranberry requires something to tame its sour taste. Toss a little rosemary spring in the mix and you have suddenly created a song you can dance to. This combination adds a delightful festival of flavors and do not fall anywhere short on the health scale.

Pork is rich in B12, B6, Thiamin (B1), Niacin (B3). What happens when you get all those B vitamins together? They convert food into fuel that gives the body a nice energy pick-me-up. Thiamine aids many body functions including the nervous system, muscle function, and helping out electrolytes by enabling them to transport themselves in and out of nerve cells, muscle cells, as well as digestion and carbohydrate metabolism. Cranberries are a good source of fiber and vitamins. They also possess high levels of proanthocyanidins that help the body fight bacteria.

Ingredients:

- 3-4 pound pork loin
- 1/4 teaspoon dried rosemary
- 1 bag frozen cranberries
- 1/2 cup apple cider or juice (unsweetened)
- 2 granny smith apples, sliced into small wedges

Method:

1. Cut your pork loin in half lengthwise.
2. Top with granny smith apple wedges, sprinkle Rosemary over the apples.
3. Layer frozen cranberries on one side of the pork loin. Fold over and tie together.
4. Add tied pork to slow cooker and pour ½ a cup of apple cider into the pot.
5. Cover the pork loin with your mixture.
6. Cook on low for 6 hours or high for 5 hours.
7. Let meat set for 2 - 3 minutes before serving.

New Castle Lamb Curry

The relationship between Britain and India began long ago. English commercial ships were used to transport exotic teas and spices back to England where both soon became a pillar of the English culinary landscape. New Castle Lamb Curry was born from these circumstances where in New Castle the spices were brought in by ship along the river Tyne. The spices caught the attention of a few local pubs whose owners began adding them to traditional meals. New Castle Lamb Curry includes a full selection of spices used back then, all of which have a number of medicinal health benefits. Lamb is high in iron, B12 and protein.

Ingredients:

- 1 ½ pound lamb
- 1 large onion, diced
- 2 garlic cloves, minced
- ½ tablespoon
- ½ tablespoon coriander
- ½ tablespoon turmeric
- ½ tablespoon cumin
- ½ tablespoon yellow mustard
- ½ tablespoon white pepper
- ½ tablespoon ginger
- ½ tablespoon cinnamon
- ½ tablespoon chilli powder
- ½ tablespoon cloves
- ½ tablespoon cardamom
- ½ tablespoon fennel
- 1 teaspoon garam masala
- Salt and pepper

Method:

1. Put the onions and garlic in the slow cooker and stir in the curry spices and garam masala.
2. Add the meat and sprinkle with a little more curry powder and some salt and pepper.
3. Cook on high 1 hour and then low 5 hours.
4. Carefully remove the meat and then puree the onions, garlic and meat juices with an immersion blender.
5. Shred the meat and debone -- return it to the crockpot.
6. Add more curry powder, salt or pepper, as needed.

Johnny Appleseed

The apple has found itself used in a variety of ways. Often it is immediately thought of as a fruit that goes with pastries and pies. As this recipe will demonstrate, that is not always the case. The appeal of apples is that that can be used to accent a great number of things. That is what early pioneers resettling to western regions of the United States learned during the 1860's while traveling along arduous trails where every now and again an oasis of apple trees would appear on the horizon.

A young man by the name, Johnny Appleseed anticipated the route droves of settlers would one day take. As apple trees sprouted their fruits, travelers bought as many as they could afford to carry. The apple eventually became synonymous with American lifestyle but not all the recipes they were used with were as popular as apple pie.

Johnny Appleseed blends juice chicken, apples, sweet potatoes and other fine indredients that have stood the test of time to bring you back to flavors enjoyed a century ago. The chicken is a wonderful source of protein and apples are bursting with vitamin C. Sweet potatoes are everyone's best friend, their properties help balance hormones and keep other vital organs in the body running as smooth as the wheel of time.

Ingredients:

- 1 ½ teaspoon whole fennel seeds
- 3 pounds boneless skinless chicken thighs
- 3 firm, sweet baking apples, cut into 6 wedges each
- 2 medium sweet potatoes (10 ounces each), cut into 1 1/2-inch chunks

- 1 large sweet onion, halved and sliced
- 2 tablespoons sliced fresh sage leaves
- 1 ¼ teaspoon fine sea salt
- ¾ teaspoon freshly ground black pepper

Method:

1. Toast fennel seeds in a small skillet over medium heat until fragrant, about 2 minutes.
2. Cut chicken thighs in half.
3. Add chicken, fennel seeds and all remaining indredients to a slow cooker.
4. Cover and cook on low until chicken and apples are very tender, 6 to 7 hours on low or 3 to 3 1/2 hours on high.
5. Let meat rest 2 - 3 minutes before serving.

Cinnamon Chuck

Cinnamon use dates back to antiquity. It was so coveted for its aromatic scent and culinary ability to accent a dish, it was considered a reasonable gift when visiting a king. At a time when Venetians controlled cinnamon trade, other western powers set out to find the secret origin of the spice. After Roman ruling parties tired of battling for cinnamon the Dutch took over its import. It is during this time that Cinnamon Chuck was born.

The Dutch were aware cinnamon was widely celebrated for its use in both for savory and sweet dishes. A chef in Amsterdam began adding it to stews during the winter months. Finally, in the case of Cinnamon Chuck, on a day in spring, the same chef featured the spice by showing off its abilities to enhance a roast with deep, earthy, warm flavors. The roast was served to the queen and king but only after the original chef appointed to cook that day did not show up for work after a long night of drinking. Cinnamon Chuck was an accidental hit. Apart from tasting good and being fast and easy to prepare, this is a great meal with many health benefits. Cinnamon and mint have a number of medicinal properties. Roast is packed with proteins.

Ingredients:

- 2 teaspoons olive oil
- 2 ½ pound beef chuck roast -- trim excess fat**
- 1 teaspoon fine sea salt
- 1/2 teaspoon ground black pepper
- 2 onions, roughly chopped

- 3 cloves garlic, thinly sliced
- 1 can diced tomatoes
- 4 cinnamon sticks
- ¼ cup finely chopped fresh mint

**trimming excess fat from meats added to a slow cooker is advised!*

Method:

1. Heat oil in a large skillet over medium-high heat. Add 1/2 teaspoon salt and 1/4 teaspoon pepper to beef surface and sear your meat until it is golden brown on all sides.
2. Transfer your seared beef to your slow cooker.
3. Add onions and garlic to skillet -- cook until caramelized.
4. Add remaining 1/2 teaspoon salt and 1/4 teaspoon pepper. Transfer onion mixture to the slow cooker along with tomatoes with their juices and finally cinnamon sticks.
5. Cover and cook until meat is fork-tender, 8 to 10 hours on low or 4 to 5 hours on high.
6. To serve, spoon sauce over meat and sprinkle with mint.
7. Let rest for 5 to 10 minutes, then slice against the grain into 1/4-inch thick slices and serve.

Chapter 6: Whole Food Slow Cooker Challenge Seafood Recipes

We are always being told to eat more fish. These recipes will pave your path and help weave them into your diet on a regular basis if you have not already. Fish are an excellent source of oils, minerals, and vitamins. Depending upon where you live, a vast variety may not be readily available for you to enjoy. We have shaped a good amount of our fish recipes to center around salomon because it is commonly widely available -- whether fresh, frozen, or farmed. We encourage not buying farmed fish because in general there is too much evidence that supports farmed fish are not in the pristine condition.

If you are like me salmon can become bland after a while. Knowing this, we have dedicated ourselves to seeking out recipes that will not compromise the Whole30 Diet and assure each salmon dish made will emerge from your slow cooker sporting a variety of flavors, smells and tastes as to avoid the sense that you are swimming upstream in the joy of eating department.

Slow cooking seafood might seem tricky at the onset. It's not. There are only two things to remember. Line your slow cooker with foil to fold around the fish and when it comes to smaller sized fish and crustaceans, calculate a time to add them (usually 30 minutes before the main fish is scheduled to be done). This will assure things like shrimp and scallops do not surface from your slow cooker tasting like flavorless chewing gum.

Additionally, we want to remind to make this seafood entrees truly spectacular, they should be mindfully paired with side dishes. This does not always mean a salad. Consider easy to prepare vegetable dishes, such as roasted carrots or corn on the cob. Just make sure it is on your list of Whole30 indredients!

***For fish dishes, aluminum foil will always be necessary. Buy some!*

The Loving Kiss

Wild Salmon Saloon was first made popular in a small southern orange grove in Florida after the owner who was an avid fisherman arrived home after a trip to Alaska with his son-in-law with several gorgeous, freshly caught salmon. He wanted to smoke all the fish but his wife intervened. They agreed to split his winnings. Three salmon were smoke while the others were cooked up and served with oranges from the couple's groves.

The man was so happy with this wife's accomplishment, he described to guests that the dish brought the tropics and far north together in a loving kiss. Raspberries were added to enhance the story, they symbolize love, passion and kissing.

Nonetheless, oranges and berries are culinarily complementary in the right company. As if you needed proof salmon is versatile! It is a healthy, hearty fish that does not have an overwhelming fishy flavor. Thus, it can stretch in as many ways as the palate inspires. In addition to the taste and amazing Method: of this dish, your plate will be brimming with the nutritional benefits of salmon. Omega-3's, Vitamin D, Vitamin B, magnesium... all of these and more are plentiful in this dish.

Ingredients:

- 4 salmon fillets
- 2 oranges, sliced
- 1 cup fresh raspberries
- 1 cup fresh orange juice
- 2 tablespoons orange zest
- ½ cup virgin olive oil
- 2 teaspoons ground coriander
- Sea salt
- Freshly ground black pepper

Method:

1. In a bowl, mix your orange juice, orange zest, ground coriander, olive oil.
2. Add your salmon fillets and marinate generous with your orange mixture --cover and refrigerate for 1 hour.
3. Add salmon filets to slow cooker by folding foil over the fish so the meat is sealed up with all of the seasoning-- do this after covering generously with orange and raspberries slices.
4. Place in your slow cooker, cover with lid and heat on high for 2 hours.
5. Let the salmon rest for 2 to 3 minutes before serving.
6. Serve the salmon with the grilled oranges, the orange-raspberry sauce.

***Long slow cooking has a tendency to toughen fish and seafood. Check fish for flakiness to determine whether it's done.*

Three By Sea Stew

Three By Sea is seafood frenzy. It is a mixture of fresh halibut, salmon, shrimp and scallions that magically transform into a warm wintry supper when in the end, tomato are added. The fish pot becomes a colorful, deep stew, that sooths the soul.

The founders of this recipe knew this which is probably why it became a traditional Newfoundland dish. The dish's origins trace back to Newfoundland where fishing villages enjoy access to a massive variety of fish and often are inspired to find creative ways to use all that they pull from the fresh sea.

In addition to the taste and amazing Method: of this dish, your plate will be brimming with the nutritional benefits of salmon. Salmon is one of the most nutrient-rich protein sources you can eat because of the Omega-3 fats and nutrients like vitamin B and selenium.

Ingredients:

- ½ pounds. halibut fillet
- ½ pounds salmon fillet
- 20 raw shrimps
- ½ pounds. sea scallops
- 2 garlic cloves, minced
- 1 small fennel pounds, diced
- ½ teaspoons . chili flakes
- 2 cups fish or chicken stock
- 2 cups tomato sauce
- 1 cup butternut squash, grated
- Juice from ½ lemon
- Olive Oil
- Sea salt
- Freshly ground black pepper

Method:

1. Remove the skins from both fishes then chop both filets into quarter-sized pieces.
2. Peeled and devein shrimp.
3. Heat olive oil in a saucepan over medium heat, add the garlic, stir until its juices flavor the oil and the fennel, and chili flakes -- cook them for 4 to 5 minutes.
4. Deglaze your pan with the fish stock -- pour in the tomato paste and grated butternut squash; bring to a boil, then lower heat.
5. Line your slow cooker with foil. Gently add your fish, generously pouring your sauce over the top and sealing the foil ---- cook on low heat for 2 hours.
6. After 2 hours, add shrimp and sea scallops, they will cook fast and adding them last will keep them supple and from getting dry -- cook for 20 - 30 minutes.
7. Let fish relax 2 - 3 minutes before serving.
8. Add in the lemon juice and season to the flavors.
9. Serve topped with lovely lime wedges.

Orange Zephyr Poach

The same couple who brings us *The Loving Kiss* created this recipe. *Orange Zephyr Poach* is named after the train the man took at the onset of his salmon fishing adventure. Again, this recipe uses oranges but it takes another direction than *The Loving Kiss*. By adding onion and dill, the outcome of this dish is zesty, earthy, and unbelievably satisfying.

It is not likely you need to be reminded that salmon is one of the most nutrient-rich protein sources you can eat because of the Omega-3 fats and nutrients like vitamin B and selenium. Oranges provide ample vitamin C.

Ingredience:

- 4 salmon fillets
- 4 oranges, sliced
- 1 yellow onion, diced
- 1 lemon, sliced
- 1 sprig of fresh dill
- ½ teaspoon salt

Method:

1. Stack a handful of oranges on each fillet and sprinkle with salt and pepper. Fold the foil over the fish so the meat is sealed up with all of the seasoning. Place in your slow cooker, cover with lid and heat on high for 2 hours.

2. For poaching, add one cup of water, one yellow onion slice, one lemon slice, one sprig of fresh dill, 1/2 teaspoon salt. Combine water and and remaining indredients. Cook on low heat for 30 mins.

3. Let the salmon rest for 2 to 3 minutes before serving.

***Long slow cooking has a tendency to toughen fish and seafood. Check fish for flakiness to determine whether it's done.

Sardina Saturday

The azure tones of the Mediterranean Sea are not unlike that of Tuna. All along the white sandy shores of the island of Sardinia are fishing villages. Each boasts of their own culinary creation. It is truly an island blessed with a deep love for food and more than food, a love of eating. Sardinia Saturday is a tuna dish that got its name simply because in most of the coastal villages locals cook up this tuna dish every Saturday.

On days when you want to get away from it all and can't, this is a nice meal to devour while you're letting your mind drift to another time and place. Of course, like all other fish, boasts high levels of Omega-3 fats and selenium, the latter an essential nutrient that supports thyroid function.

Ingredients:

- 4 tuna steaks
- 1 teaspoons cumin
- 1 teaspoons paprika
- 2 garlic cloves, minced
- ¼ cup olive oil
- Juice from 1 lime
- ½ cup fresh cilantro, chopped
- 1 tablespoons hot pepper sauce
- Sea salt
- Fresh ground black pepper

Method:

1. In a bowl combine the cumin, paprika, minced garlic, olive oil, lime juice, cilantro, and hot pepper sauce.
2. Line your slow cooker with foil. Season the tuna steaks to taste with sea salt and freshly ground black pepper.
3. Brush the seasoned tuna steaks generously with with the cilantro-lime sauce.
4. Wrap tuna in foil. Set your slow cooker to low for 2 hours.
5. Let rest 2 to 3 minutes before serving.
6. Serve with lime wedges.

South Pacific Blue Song

The South Pacific Blue Song is named after a songbird that sings whenever this meal is being prepared and eaten in the south pacific. The inexplicable incident was first noted by a fisherman who after spending years at sea became enamored by the song when he was preparing his evening meal. He was familiar enough with bird behavior to know he could expect the same serenade the following night at the same hour which is when he normally cooked his dinner.

Night after night, the song went unsung until a long time had passed and he finally heard it again. This continued until over a year had passed. The fishman told his young son the story. Unable to understand the irregularly of the bird's will to sing, both the fisherman and his son shared cooking duties hoping they might together figure out why the bird did not sing every evening. After a few months on a night the bird sang to them, while eating the son realized the answer. He told his father, the bird only sings when we make this dish.

Obviously, the two put the hypothesis to test the following night. When the bird's song flooded their ears they were overjoyed. They wanted to name the recipe the bird sang to after the event and not the bird as to not give away the bird's identity.

Meanwhile, they did not keep the identity of the recipe the bird sings to a secret. It is a spectacular blend of zesty indredients. In addition to the taste and easy Method: of this dish, your plate will be brimming with the nutritional benefits of salmon. Salmon is one of the most nutrient-rich protein sources you can eat because of the Omega-3 fats and nutrients like vitamin B and selenium.

Ingredients:

- 4 salmon fillets
- 1 ripe avocado
- 1/3 cup coconut milk**
- 1/4 cup fresh cilantro minced
- 1 tablespoons fresh lime juice
- 1 teaspoons garlic
- 1 tablespoon lime zest

**To assure it is whole30, use coconut milk with no sulfites

Method:

1. Season the salmon fillets and generously sprinkle with zest of lime.
2. Line your slow cooker with foil, add the salmon, fold paper. Cook for 2 hours on low.
3. In a bowl, add your avocado, coconut milk, cilantro, lime juice, garlic powder, salt and pepper in a blender or food processor and pulse until sauce is creamy -- add more coconut milk to attain desired creaminess.
4. Let the salmon rest for 2 to 3 minutes before serving.
5. Serve the salmon topped with avocado-coconut sauce, and top with lime wedges.

***Long slow cooking has a tendency to toughen fish and seafood. Check fish for flakiness to determine whether it's done

Turbulent Harold

Cloves are not a run of the mill ingredient when it comes to fish which is why this recipe caught our attention. Also, the recipe which came to us from a remote village in Maine has humor behind it. Whenever the fishermen inquire at the end of the day about their catch, Halibut are referred to as "Harold." If netted Harold is easy to deal with until he is lured onto the boat. If by pole, Harold is known for giving even the most seasoned fishman a run for his money. The fish can get quite big and evidently resist every attempt to be caught. Also, Harold is the name of a local who could not keep out of trouble and despite being caught by the police, a number of times managed to sneak out of jail.

Halibut Harold is high in B6, B12, and D vitamins as well as magnesium. Both it and clove are an incredible source of potassium. Cloves are surprisingly high in calcium and fiber.

Ingredients:

- 4 halibut filets
- 2 tablespoons olive oil
- 4 garlic cloves, minced
- 1 tablespoon lemon zest
- 1 lemon sliced
- 2 tablespoons fresh cilantro, minced
- Sea salt
- Fresh ground black pepper

Method:

1. Combine the olive oil, garlic, lemon zest, lemon juice, and parsley; season with salt and pepper to taste.
2. Prepare slow cooker with foil, add your fish and then smother fish with your mix; top with fresh lemon slices. Seal foil tightly.
3. Set slow cooker for 2 hours on low heat.
4. Serve the fish topped with cilantro and lemon wedges.

Lustrous Lucy

Lustrous Lucy is a Californian favorite. The recipe comes from San Diego which geographically is located incredibly near the Mexican border, so much so, the culinary worlds of both countries have been colliding their for decades. The result is a cuisine that has not yet been named despite having clear qualifiers that make it neither North American nor Mexican.

You will understand what we mean when you make Lustrous Lucy. It exemplifies a fusion of both cultures, salmon being American and indredients like lime, cilantro having attributes that clearly were not not used unless when near the Mexican border. Clove are an incredible source of potassium. Cloves are surprisingly high in calcium and fiber. Salmon is one of the most nutrient-rich protein sources you can eat because of the Omega-3 fats and nutrients like vitamin B and selenium.

Ingredients:

- 2 salmon filets
- ¼ cup olive oil
- 4 garlic cloves, minced
- 4 lemons, sliced
- Juice from 1 lime
- ¼ cup fresh cilantro, minced
- 2 fresh rosemary sprigs
- Sea salt and freshly ground black pepper

Method (Salmon Fillets):

1. Preheat grill to medium heat.
2. In a bowl, combine olive oil, lime juice, garlic, and fresh parsley; season with salt and pepper to taste.
3. Brush the salmon fillets generously with the garlic-lime sauce.
4. Place the lemon slices tightly together on the grill, forming a flat layer.
5. Place the salmon fillets on top of the lemon slices, top with fresh rosemary sprigs, and grill 15 to 20 minutes, or until fish is cooked through and no longer pink.

Anarchy in Anchoridge

Anarchy in Anchorage is how locals who lay claim to the last frontier by calling it home define the Alaskan lifestyle. With few people and vastly diverse and massive amount of land the idea of anarchy departs from its politically charged roots. In Alaska, anarchy is about learning how to survive with and from the wilderness where behaviors that make sense in other parts of the world do not apply. For example, we were reminded, you cannot take a bear to court and sue him if he eats you.

Within the wilderness of the Alaskan lust for life, one can find scores of ripe blackberries bursting with flavor. Mixing those with salmon and a dash of ginger may not be an act of anarchy but eating it might be. Salmon is one of the most nutrient-rich protein sources you can eat because of the Omega-3 fats and nutrients like vitamin B and selenium. Blackberries are an ideal source of antioxidants and vitamin C.

Ingredients:

- 4 salmon filets
- 2 garlic cloves, minced
- 1 tablespoons fresh ginger, minced
- 2 cups fresh blackberries
- 2 tablespoons . coconut oil**
- Sea salt
- freshly ground black pepper

To assure it is whole30, use coconut milk with no sulfites

Method:

1. Melt coconut oil in a skillet over medium heat.
2. Season the salmon filets to taste with sea salt and freshly ground black pepper.
3. Fry the filets in the skillet 2 to 3 minutes per side, or until nicely browned, and set aside.
4. Add the garlic and ginger and cook 1 to 2 minutes.
5. Add in the blackberries and cook another 1 to 2 minutes.
6. Bring the salmon back to the pan and cook 6 to 8 minutes, spooning the sauce on top every minute or so.
7. Serve the salmon filets topped with the blackberry sauce.

Paris Paella

Tremendous sophistication at peasant prices, is what the French call Paris Paella. It is a communal dish that is commonly shared -- liken to soup -- wherein everyone who is at the table dishes up a scoop adding it to their plate. This recipe originates from south of France, in Spain. It is called Paris Paella because Parisians traveling through the Pyrenees Mountains were known for talking about it after eating it along their arduous journey. This caused the Spanish living at the Pyrenees foothills to begin traveling into the mountains to try the magically meal themselves which is how we happened upon it.

Sticking with our desire to bring to a number of ways to prepare salmon, we will remind you it is one of the most nutrient-rich protein sources you can eat because of the Omega-3 fats and nutrients like vitamin B and selenium.

Ingredients:

- ¾ c. chopped sweet peppers
- ½ c. chopped onion
- 2 cloves garlic, minced
- 2 ½ cups chicken broth**
- ½ teaspoons thyme
- ¼ teaspoons crushed red pepper
- ¼ teaspoons ground turmeric
- 12 oz. fresh or frozen shrimp, thawed, peeled and halved
- 6 oz. canned or pouched wild-caught pink salmon, flaked
- 1 c. frozen peas

**Make sure chicken broth meets Whole30 standards and is not high in sodium (check the label carefully).*

Method:

1. Grease your slow cooker with olive oil.
2. Add all veggies except peas.
3. In a medium saucepan, combine chicken broth and spices.
4. Heat until boiling, then pour over veggies in the crock pot.
5. Cover and cook on low for 4 hours.
6. After about 3 hours, add the shrimp, salmon and peas.
7. Let stand for 10 minutes to let indredients settle before serving.

Bombasity by the Bay

This is a flavorful stew with marinated tilapia, bell peppers, tomatoes, and onions in a coconut milk broth. The name is inspired by the use of tilapia. It is a fish known for its lightness, both in flavor and texturally, so much so, you can cook nearly anything imaginable with is and churn out a spectacular dish. It is a fish that gives more than it gives as the saying goes.

Tilapia is high in omegas, bell peppers and tomatoes in vitamin C.

Ingredients:

- 4 tablespoons lime juice
- 1 and ½ tablespoons ground cumin
- 1 and ½ tablespoons paprika
- 2 and ½ teaspoons minced garlic
- 1 and ½ teaspoons salt
- 1 and ½ teaspoons pepper
- 2 pounds tilapia fillets, cut into bite-sized pieces (can be frozen, just thaw slightly to cut)
- 1 tablespoon olive oil
- 1 large onion, chopped
- 3 large bell peppers, sliced into 2 inch strips
- 1 can diced tomatoes, drained
- 1 can coconut milk**
- A handful fresh cilantro, chopped

**To assure it is whole30, use coconut milk with no sulfites

Method:

1. Combine the lime juice, cumin, paprika, garlic, salt, and pepper in a large bowl--add the tilapia and mix until coated.
2. Place everything in your slow cooker.
3. Pour the coconut milk over everything, cover, and leave to simmer on low.
4. Before serving, stir in cilantro.

Chapter 7: Whole Food Slow Cooker Challenge Soup Recipes

Soups are a slow cooker's best friend! As we mentioned in the introduction, in general, soups and stews are often incredible fast and effortless. You can toss in all the required indredients in without fussing over them much, if at all. We have put together a collection of soup recipes that are sure to inspire you.

The best days to turn to soup is when the weather turns chilly and cold and you desire a pick-me-up that will warm you from head to toe --- alternatively, when you haven't the energy to think about cooking or simply are not in the mood to fuss with a lot of Method: (we all have these days!) soups are your answer! They are forgiving, fast, nutritious, easy to make and appeal to the most finicky of eaters.

Soups also make excellent appetisers. On days when you feel like creating a decadent dining extravaganza feast that will send friend's into a state of denial that *this* can possibly be part of your diet, start everyone with a small bowl of savory soup to ease their appetites into a hyper awake state. Follow up with seafood or a meat based dish with flavors you find are complimentary.

Cornwall Jubilee

End of summers in Cornwall have a special feel about them. Sunsets offer a brilliant storm of August tones. Nights slowly become cooler. The smell from the kitchen billows with a mixture of scents accenting that the season is getting ready to change.

Cornwall Jubilee is an inspired blend that is made from a variety of fish and late summer garden vegetables. If you have squash in your kitchen you cannot imagine putting to good use, this is your recipe. Of course, you will have to decide the best way to go about obtaining your fish. If you have access to fresh seafood, that is an ideal option. However, if you are landlocked, don't panic. Salmon, halibut, scallops and shrimp are all available frozen. We only caution against buying farmed fish as it has become impossible to distinguish those that are feed well against those that are not.

Ingredients:

- ½ pound halibut fillet, skinless, chopped
- ½ pound salmon fillet, skinless, chopped
- 20 raw shrimps, peeled and deveined
- ½ pound sea scallops
- 1 red onion, diced
- 2 garlic cloves, minced
- 2 carrots, diced
- 1 small fennel bulb, diced
- ½ tablespoon. chili flakes
- 2 cups fish or chicken stock
- 2 cups tomato sauce
- 1 cup butternut squash, grated
- Juice from 1/2 lemon
- Sea salt and freshly ground black pepper

Method:

1. If your fish is frozen, take them out of your freezer to thaw.
2. Add your garlic cloves, carrots, butternut squash, lemon and fennel to your slow cooker. In a bowl, empty your tomato sauce and stir in your chili flakes along with your stock cubes. Stir until cubes are dissolved. Add sauce to your slow cooker.
3. Add ¼ cup of water. Set your slow cooker on low heat for 2 hours.
4. Add fish to slow cooker on low heat for 40 mins.
5. Serve!

Lisbon by the Sea

Lisbon by the Sea ignites one's appetite by offering a mixture of spicy sausage and soothing broth. It is a hearty, thick soup that falls short of being a stew. It compliments almost any meal due to its vast array of Ingredients, all of which were inspired by Portuguese landscapes.

Ingredients:

- 3 ½ cup vegetable broth**
- 1 large green bell pepper, diced
- 1 onion, diced
- 3 cloves garlic, finely chopped
- ⅛ teaspoon crushed red pepper flakes
- ⅛ teaspoon fine sea salt
- 1 diced cherry tomatoes
- 6 spicy andouille sausage
- 1 pound kale or other hearty greens, tough stems and ribs removed, leaves sliced
- ¼ cup chopped mixed fresh herbs: parsley, thyme, basil, oregano, chives

**Vegetable broth, use only low sodium*

Method:

1. In a large saucepan, combine andouille sausage, broth, bell pepper, onion, garlic, pepper flakes and salt; bring to a boil over high heat.
2. Cover pan, lower heat until mixture just simmers and cook, stirring occasionally, until tender, about 20 minutes.
3. Add tomatoes and kale and continue to cook.
4. Serve topped with herbs.

Coconut Grove

Many Thai dishes are somewhat complex to make. Coconut Grove is not one of those dishes! It is easy and fast and divine to eat, partly because it is smooth and savory. It is also very healthy. At its base is chicken broth and butternut squash. Both are accented by coconut milk's luscious splendor.

Ingredients:

- 2 cups coconut milk**
- 2 pounds of turkey breast, cooked and chopped
- 2 cups chicken broth**
- 2 cups butternut squash, peeled and cubed
- 1 cup fresh green beans, cut (frozen are fine, too)
- 1 red bell pepper, chopped
- 1 medium onion, diced
- 2 tablespoon red curry paste
- 1 tablespoon fresh ginger, grated
- 1 lime, cut into wedges
- Optional Garnish: Baby Spinach

*To assure it is Whole30, use coconut milk with no sulfites
*Chicken broth, use only low sodium

Method:

1. Toss everything but the lime into the crock pot.
2. Cover and cook on high for 3-5 hours or on low for 5-7 hours or until the vegetables are nice and tender.
3. Serve with a wedge or two of lime and some pea shoots if desired.

Creamy Dreamy

Creamy Dreamy originated in Portland, Oregon. A state that is nearly constantly blanketed with drizzly weather, this soup was inspired by a local cafe that wanted to boost people's day by offering them something both zesty and soothing. With its chicken broth base, the soup has the same properties as Chicken Soup and can help the body fight off viruses in the body by keeping a person hydrated and well nourished and maybe even a little happy even if the forecast calls for more rain.

Ingredients:

- 1 large yellow onion, diced
- 2 carrots, peeled and diced
- 1 red pepper, diced
- 3 cups fresh or frozen corn kernels, washed and strained
- 3-4 sweet potatoes, peeled and chopped into pieces
- 2 cups chicken broth**
- 2 teaspoons garlic powder
- 2 cups almond milk**
- Salt to season
- ½ cup diced bacon --trimmed of fat

**To assure it is Whole30, use coconut milk with no sulfites
**Chicken broth, use only low sodium

Method:

1. Sear chicken in a skillet or pan over medium heat to brown all over.
2. Transfer chicken to your slow cooker or instant pot bowl.
3. Add the diced onion, carrots, red peppers, corn, sweet potatoes, chicken broth and garlic powder.
4. Stir and cover with lid; cook on slow cooker high setting for 3-4 hours or low setting 6-8 hours.
5. Stir in salt and pepper to taste; add in the cheese; top with the bacon; garnish with fresh chives and serve.

Berlin Beer Garden Soup

During long, cold, wet winters during the Cold War era gave East Germans reasons to find recipes that would cut through a chill that seemed at moments would never leave. Berlin Beer Garden Soup is a recipe that took shape between a group of friends having a beer together along the Spree River in a popular biergarden. Despite not having a lot of resources to work with, they introduced this tasty, inexpensive soup that is easy to make and connects one to the past.

Ingredients:

- 4 beefsteak tomatoes, sliced
- 2 cups cannellini beans, drained and rinsed
- 3 cups thinly sliced green cabbage
- 1 pound white sweet potatoes, cubed
- 1 onion, diced
- 5 cloves garlic, sliced
- ⅛ teaspoon crushed red chile flakes
- 2 tablespoons chopped fresh herbs

Method:

1. Preheat the slow cooker to high heat.
2. Add onions and garlic and cook until just golden brown, about 5 minutes. Add tomatoes, beans, cabbage, sweet potatoes and chile flakes along with 2 cups water to the slow cooker.
3. Cover and cook until sweet potatoes are very tender, 7 to 8 hours on low or 3 1/2 to 4 hours on high.
4. Stir in herbs.

Hobo Chicken Soup

It's warm.
It's hearty.
It's healthy.
It's everything that makes you think of "home" when you are not there.

Hobo Chicken Soup rose in popularity during the Great Depression. Throughout the 1930's, food was scarce. A lot of people took to the highways. Over time, informal Method:s were employed to signal where food could be found. A desolate farm in Indiana it was well-known stop for many travelers, some they say traveled only for the soup that was served there.

Chicken is high in protein and the assorted vegetables that accompany it in this soup offer vitamin C and D. Chicken soup is thought to be cleansing. When plenty of fluids is advised for a body that is ill. When a virus is present and the body is battling antibodies, it needs to be flushed in order to get healthy. The soup is also said to disinfect due to its salt content, which cleans the nose and throat and sinuses.

Ingredients:

- 5 cups chicken broth 5-6 cups water
- 2 cups carrots, sliced thin
- 1 cup celery, sliced thin
- 1 small onion, finely chopped
- 2 garlic cloves, minced
- ½ teaspoon dried basil
- 1 teaspoon pepper
- 2-3 pounds boneless skinless chicken breast

Method:

1. Mix all indredients in your slow cooker.
2. Keep chicken breast whole (or use pre-cooked, cut up or shredded chicken) and cut up or shred.
3. Cook on high 4 hours, then turn to low until ready to serve.

Warhol Soup

Turning the tide on Andy Warhol's use of advertising in art, this recipe places Andy Warhol in a soup -- as much as possible. Warhol Soup is a New York City meal with attitude that originated in a cafe near the famous Studio 54 nightclub that hosted a selection of celebrities throughout the 1970's and 1980's. The cafe did not begin making the soup until Studio 54 lost its pizzazz. It pays homage to an exciting time that is easy to be nostalgic for. And the soup is nostalgic in other ways, it will no doubt remind many of you of Campbell's vegetable soup you had growing up, only as you are making the soup yourself you can count on it not having a ton of sodium. Instead, this soup is made from an abundance of nutrients due to its incredibly high vegatable count.

Ingredients:
- 1 cup diced carrot
- 1 1/2 cup diced zucchini
- ¾ cup green peas
- 1 ½ cups roughly chopped kale, loosely packed
- 8 ounces sausages, sliced into coins
- ¼ teaspoon cracked black pepper
- ½ teaspoon sea salt
- ½ teaspoon garlic powder

Method:

1. Combine all indredients except zucchini and peas in your slow cooker.
2. Set on low for 3 - 4 hours.
3. Add peas and zucchini into the soup 30 minutes before serving.
4. Enjoy warm or let cool completely.

Timbuktu

This recipe is commonly eaten when en route to Timbuktu. The soup is made from indredients popular in the region but has been slightly altered to adhere to the Whole30 guidelines. Try it on day 31 with some couscous if you have an interest to indulge in the authentic version of the recipe, which is brimming with nutrients that are not only healthy, they will keep a body that is on the go moving.

Ingredients:

- 2 ½ cups diced tomatoes
- 1 small yellow onion (about 1/2 cup)
- ¾ cup diced carrots
- ½ cup diced celery
- 3 cups chicken broth**
- 1 tablespoon turmeric
- 1 teaspoon sea salt
- ½ teaspoon black pepper
- ½ teaspoon dried oregano
- 1 tablespoon dried basil
- 1 can coconut milk**

***To assure it is Whole30, use coconut milk with no sulfites*
***Chicken broth, use only low sodium*

Method:

1. Combine everything except coconut milk in your slow cooker. Stir.
2. Cover and cook on high for 4 hours or on low for 6 hours.

3. Once the soup is done cooking, use an immersion blender to puree the soup until it is very smooth and all of the vegetable chunks pieces are blended.

4. Add the coconut milk to the soup, blending or stirring for a minute or two to combine.

5. Enjoy with a little olive oil and additional salt and pepper to taste.

Genuine Ginger and Carrot Soup

Ginger Rogers loved carrot soup. This recipe combines both ginger and carrots to pay tribute to the Hollywood legend, which is from where the recipe originated. Its indredients are a rich fusion of soft and intense flavors, much like the actress. Carrots are nourishing and packed with carotene along with a number of vitamins.

Instructions:

- 2 tablespoons coconut oil**
- 1 yellow onion, peeled and diced
- 2 cloves garlic, peeled and minced
- 2 pounds carrots, washed and roughly chopped
- 4 cups broth
- 1 tablespoon fresh grated ginger
- 1 can coconut milk**
- Salt
- Pepper to taste

**To assure it is Whole30, use coconut milk with no sulfites
**Chicken broth, use only low sodium

Method:

1. In your skillet, heat the coconut oil over low heat. Once the oil is hot, add onions and garlic to the pot. Saute until onions are slightly translucent -- about 5 minutes.

2. Add your sauce and carrots, broth and ginger to your slow cooker. Set on low heat for 3-4 hours.

3. Once carrots are soft enough, use an immersion blender puree soup until smooth.

4. When the soup is creamy, stir in coconut milk. Taste and add salt and pepper to taste.

5. Enjoy immediately!

Sweet Clementine

Memphis does not just serve up good music, it has a hot selection of food that will leave you aching for more. Such is the case with Sweet Clementine. The recipe fuses the sweet, nutrient packed sweet potato and sets it on fire with chili powder. The Blues is inspired from love and hate, this soup reflects these emotions by being sweet as fire!

Ingredients:

- 2 pounds ground beef
- 1 onion, diced
- 1 clove garlic, minced
- 2 cans of tomato sauce
- 1 can of petite minced tomatoes
- 3 cups beef stock**
- 2 large sweet potatoes, peeled and diced
- 3 tablespoons chili powder
- 2 teaspoon salt
- ½ teaspoon black pepper
- ¼ teaspoon oregano
- cilantro, for garnish

Method:

1. In a saute pan, brown beef over medium heat until cooked through. Drain excess fat. As you know, fat and slow cookers do not mix.

2. Transfer cooked beef to slow cooker. Add remaining indredients to slow cooker. Stir to combine.
3. Set to cook on low for 6-8 hours // high 3-4 hours. Stir to break up the meat and serve warm!
4. Garnish with cilantro.

Plume

This recipe beacons from the small mountain village of Silver Plume, Colorado where you would have to know a local to find this cafe because it is actually inside a storefront converted into a living space. That does not stop those who live there from cooking up a feast and inviting everyone around. It also does not stop everyone around from freely dropping in when they are hungry which is why there is always a pot boiling with Plume Soup on the stovetop.

Ingredients:

- 2 cups dried lentils, rinsed and looked over
- 2 cans diced tomatoes
- 1 cup chopped onion
- 1 cup chopped carrot
- 1 can chilies
- 5 cups chicken broth **
- 1 teaspoon salt
- 1 teaspoon oregano
- 1 teaspoon thyme
- ½ teaspoon garlic powder
- ¼ teaspoon pepper

**Chicken broth, use only low sodium*

Method:

1. Combine all indredients in a 4-5 quart crock pot.
2. Cover and cook on low for 8-9 hours or until lentils are tender.
3. Serve with a dollop of yogurt and salt.

Chapter 8: Whole Food Slow Cooker Challenge Salad Recipes

Crunchy, fresh, juicy, rejuvenating -- salads are easy to make when you are on the go. They are often incredibly quick to make and they are forgiving. If you are missing an ingredient -- even if it's a key ingredient -- you can often get away with exchanging it for something else or nothing at all!

Apart from being easy to make and not being time consumptive, salads have been a celebrated source of vital vitamins, minerals, and proteins. For centuries humans have eaten them. Most notably, they include staple ingredients that make up the Mediterranean Diet.

If you are not familiar, the Mediterranean Diet is made primarily of leafy greens, vegetables, fruits, fish, and olive oil. This diet has stood out to the science community since the 1940's when it was discovered that those whose diets consist mainly of these foods live to be very, very old. Not being able to pinpoint the link between the Mediterranean Diet and longevity has long baffled scientists. At least, it did until recently. A comprehensive study finally concluded that it is the mixture of olive oil and leafy greens that are driving force behind what makes the Mediterranean Diet a beacon of health.

When olive oil is drizzled over leafy greens, a chemical reaction happens. This chemical reaction produces amazing effects that enable our bodies to drive out anything nasty. This is believed to be the reason Italy has lower rates of cancer than other countries and to be the reason Italians living in regions where the Mediterranean Diet is prevalent live to a ripe old age.

Calamari Farm Salad

Calamari Farm Salad is like eating a song. It is only popular in small villages along cooler coastal regions of New England. When berry season peaks between late July through the beginning of September, local fishermen and berry farmers brazenly began mixing the catch of the day with the seasonal berry. Calamari became a favored fish for the salad probably due to its subtle flavors. While it is a domineering ingredient, its taste does not dominate the salad.

It is a healthy treat, calamari is rich in B vitamins, especially B2 and B12. It's also rich in minerals like copper and selenium. The B's are always vital to get into one's diet. Copper and selenium support the body in a number of ways, including healthy cell production. Blueberries not only burst with sweet and sour charm, they are one of the few blue foods in the world. Add to that unique outer tonality, they are an excellent antioxidant as are cranberries.

Almonds and apples go hand in hand. Both are good for keeping the body's insides moving along. Almonds not only have a full natural taste, they also aid in digestion.

Ingredients:

- 1-½ pounds calamari tubes, (cleaned)
- ¼ cup extra virgin olive oil
- ½ lemon
- 1 granny smith apple, thinly sliced
- 6 cups fresh spinach
- ¾ cup blueberries
- ¼ cup dried cranberries (unsweetened)
- ¼ cup sliced almonds
- Sea salt
- Fresh ground black pepper

Ingredients (Dressing):

- ¼ cup extra virgin olive oil
- 2 tablespoon apple cider vinegar
- 1 tablespoon fresh lemon juice
- Sea salt and freshly ground black pepper

Method:

1. Preheat grill on medium heat.
2. Combine olive oil, lemon juice, and season with salt and pepper.
3. Baste your calamari tubes with the olive-lemon mixture.
4. Now, you are ready to grill the tubes. Usually, this takes a short time -- about 2 minutes per side.
5. When they are done, set them aside and slice them lengthwise.
6. In a bowl, combine all the indredients for the dressing and whisk until well blended.
7. In a salad bowl combine all the salad indredients and drizzle the dressing.
8. Gingerly toss until covered.

Peach and White Fish Salad

By August the state of Georgia is afloat with peach trees are bountiful in this region due to the climate and mineral rich soil. Not far away from the countryside is the city of Charleston where cafes are bustling inside historic buildings erected in the 1700's. Tradition is a prized possession in this region which might explain why it is not difficult to get one's hands on recipes from Georgia's past.

Peach and White Fish Salad is one of the recipes. Its indredients tell the story of the state's history. Fish and peaches make up a huge portion of Georgia's food production. It is no wonder they should fall from time to time in the same dish. What's unique about this particular recipe is the peaches and fish are served warm in cold bed of greens. It is a situation not until a warm summer day in the heart of Georgia, where things can be both hot and cold at the same time. Fish are loaded with omega-3's, Vitamin D, Vitamin B, magnesium and peaches with vitamin C. That both taste good and are complementary to one another will indeed make this one of those dishes that, like Georgia, stays on your mind.

Ingredients:

- 1 ½ pounds white fish fillets
- 2 to 3 peaches, sliced
- 6 cups mixed greens
- 1 quarter sized fresh ginger, minced
- 2 green onions, sliced
- 2 garlic cloves, minced
- ¼ cup lime juice
- ½ cup olive oil
- 2 tablespoon balsamic vinegar

- 1 teaspoon chili flakes
- ¼ cup pine nuts, toasted
- Cooking fat
- Sea salt
- Fresh ground black pepper

Method:

1. In a bowl, combine the olive oil, lime juice, balsamic vinegar, green onions, garlic, ginger, and chili flakes; season to taste with salt and pepper.
2. Divide the mixture in half and brush the white fish fillets with half of the sauce.
3. Melt some cooking fat in a skillet over medium-high heat, and cook the peaches until soft, 2 to 3 minutes per side.
4. Set the peaches aside, add some more olive oil to the skillet, and cook the fish 4 to 5 minutes per side, until done.
5. Serve the fish and peaches on top of the mixed greens.
6. Drizzle the salad with the remaining dressing, top with toasted pine nuts, and serve.

Sunset Strip

The Sunset Strip is a fusion of foods rich in protein, omega-3's, Vitamin D, Vitamin B, magnesium and everything else a body need when seeking something refreshing, filling and holistically beneficial. It should come as no surprise the recipe was developed in California's sunny Los Angeles. Avocados are bursting with vitamin K as well as B6, C, and E. They are a rich source of potassium and magnesium. There are over 20 minerals and vitamins in these tropical gems, so instead of listing them all we are just going to remind you, avocados are good to eat!

Combined with eggs and salmon, this sassy salad is perfect if in the mood for a cosmopolitan social scene or from a quiet remote place where one can watch a lingering, romantic sunset.

Ingredients:

- 2 cups flaked salmon, cooked
- 2 hard boiled eggs, diced
- 1 bell pepper, diced
- 1 avocado, diced
- ½ red onion, minced
- ¼ cup homemade mayonnaise
- ¼ teaspoon cayenne pepper
- Juice from half lemon
- ¼ cup.fresh parsley, minced
- 2 tablespoon olive oil
- Sea salt and freshly ground black pepper

Method:

1. In a bowl, whisk the mayonnaise, parsley, lemon juice, cayenne and olive oil, until well emulsified.
2. In a salad bowl add the salmon, diced eggs, bell pepper, avocado, and red onion.
3. Pour the mayonnaise mixture over the salmon mixture.
4. Toss everything gently until well mixed.
5. Get ready to eat

Del Mar

They can be boiled, broiled, baked, grilled or lightly fried in coconut oil for a more exotic flavor. Shrimp are a versatile seafood that can be altered to fit any mood your appetite goes in. Plus, they are high in vitamin E and magnesium. Both these are mood boosters -- so is sitting seaside, which is where this salad takes its inspiration.

Along the coastal regions of Mexico are plentiful bays filled with a diverse selection of fish. Not unlike the sea, the country is known for its agricultural diversity. During the springtime when flowers are in bloom and fruit trees are wildly blossoming, the village of Del Mar celebrates by serving this exquisite salad using fresh sea shrimp and avocados from nearby orchards.

Add avocado to their side and you have a party going on! Avocados are bursting with vitamin K as well as B6, C, and E. They are a rich source of potassium and magnesium. There are over 20 minerals and vitamins in these tropical gems, so instead of listing them all we are just going to remind you, avocados are good to eat!

Ingredients (salad):

- 1 lb. shrimp, deveined and shelled
- 1 teaspoon minced garlic
- Juice of ½ lemon
- Pinch of salt
- Head of lettuce
- Cubed avocado
- Chopped fresh tomato

Ingredients (dressing):

- 1 tablespoon red wine vinegar
- 1 tablespoon lemon juice
- 2 tablespoon olive oil
- Salt & pepper to taste

Method:

1. In your skillet add the shrimp and fry until cooked through -- about 2-5 minutes.
2. Add the garlic, lemon juice and salt to the shrimp and fry for another 30 seconds. Remove and set aside.
3. Add your avocado, tomato, shrimp and on a bed of lettuce, then drizzle the dressing over it all. Toss and serve.

Lemon Tango Shrimp

Do you want a salad that raises the bar? Well, your ship has come in! Lemon Shrimp tango is a sophisticated mix. Because its core ingredient is lobster, we recommend this as a spring or summer offering. Of course, that does not mean you cannot enjoy it in any season you choose!

Lemon Shrimp Tango was popular in the 1930's among a small crowd whose summer vacations included sipping gin on the front porch of mansion sized beach homes lining the shores of Jekyll Island, Georgia. Mangos grown in Florida were transported up the coast while lobster from Maine were moved to the deep south. It is highly advisable to invite your friends over and keep the tradition alive. This salad tends to seduce even the most finicky eaters.

Something to know about lobster is that it is loaded with selenium, which protects cell damage. Lobster is also loaded with proteins. Along with lobster, eggs add balance to this salad, nourishing it with equal parts protein, fat and carbs. Eggs also act as a source of vitamins A and C and iron. Meanwhile, mango is an excellent source of vitamins, it stands out as a rich source of vitamin C.

Method: of this salad does not take much time. You may notice that these ingredients are not often used together. Let me tell you a secret, that is the reason this salad stands out! Surprise your family and friends offering them a breath of fresh air!

Ingredients (salad):

- 6 oz. cooked lobster meat, chopped
- 1 mango, peeled and diced
- 2 hard-boiled eggs, chopped
- ½ cup grape tomatoes, halved
- 1 head romaine lettuce, chopped

Ingredients (dressing):

- ¼ cup extra-virgin olive oil
- 2 tablespoon apple cider vinegar
- 1 tablespoon fresh lemon juice
- 1 teaspoon Dijon mustard
- 1 clove garlic, minced
- Sea salt and freshly ground black pepper

Method:

1. Combine all the indredients for the dressing, season to taste with salt and pepper, and whisk until well blended.
2. Ready the salad on two plates by topping the chopped romaine with the lobster meat, mango, boiled eggs, and grape tomatoes.
3. Drizzle the salad with the dressing, gently toss, sprinkle fresh parsley, and serve.

Tucson Tracy

Tucson Tracy salad is fresh, zesty and spirited. The story behind the salad's origins link to a woman left her corporate career. Without knowing what to do next, she climbed in her car and began driving. Her car broke down in Tucson, Arizona where she began frequenting a local cafe. The owner made her a special salad that he felt captured a woman who made herself free. Avocados are bursting with vitamin K as well as B6, C, and E. They are a rich source of potassium and magnesium. There are over 20 minerals and vitamins in these tropical gems, so instead of listing them all we are just going to remind you, avocados are good to eat!

Ingredients:

- 2 cups cooked and flaked tuna
- 1 English cucumber, diced
- 1 to 2 avocados, diced
- ½ red onion, sliced
- ¼ cup fresh cilantro, minced
- 2 tablespoon fresh lemon juice
- ¼ cup extra virgin olive oil
- ½ teaspoon paprika (optional)
- Sea salt and freshly ground black pepper

Method:

1. In a small bowl combine the cilantro, lemon juice, olive oil, and season to taste with salt and pepper.

2. In a larger bowl combine the tuna, cucumber, avocado, and red onion.

3. Drizzle the vinaigrette over the salad and toss everything gently.

4. Sprinkle the paprika over the salad if using, and refrigerate until ready to eat.

Easy Green Forest

Sometimes simple is best. Easy Green Forest combines tasty ingredients that complement one another. The soft, supple elegance and vitamin rich avocado next to sunflower seeds explodes. The contrast between crunchiness and cream make this salad a sensational experience. Eggs add balance to this salad, nourishing it with equal parts protein, fat and carbs. Eggs also act as a source of vitamins A and C and iron.

Of course, Avocados are bursting with vitamin K as well as B6, C, and E. They are a rich source of potassium and magnesium. There are over 20 minerals and vitamins in these tropical gems, so instead of listing them all we are just going to remind you, avocados are good to eat!

Ingredients:

- 1 bag of greens
- ¼ red onion, diced
- 1 large tomato, seeded and diced
- ⅓ cup roasted sunflower seeds
- 1 ripe avocado, thinly sliced
- 2 eggs, soft boiled
- Salt & pepper to taste

Ingredients (dressing):

- ¼ cup olive oil
- 3 tbs apple cider vinegar
- 1 tablespoons dijon mustard
- juice of 1 lemon

Method:

1. Combine olive oil, cider vinegar, mustard, and lemon-- whisk.
2. Fill a salad bowl with a mixture of greens, onion, seeds, eggs, and avocado.
3. Pour dressing.
4. Salt and pepper.
5. Serve!

Alvarado Island Salad

Alvarado Island Salad is so good it's dizzying. Its zucchini base is loaded with minerals. In particular, we are talking about magnesium, which offers a wealth of contribution. Magnesium supports the muscles (including the heart muscles) and it is a natural mood elevator. This is why people who spend time in natural hot springs found in western states such as Washington and Colorado feel invigorated afterward. The spring water is high in magnesium! Eating foods rich in this mineral has a similar effect. Eggs adds balance to this salad, nourishing it with equal parts protein, fat and carbs. Eggs also act as a source of vitamins A and C and iron.

Ingredients:

- 2 small zucchini or 1 large zucchini
- ½ avocado
- ¼ cup olive oil
- 2 tbsp water
- 1-2 garlic cloves
- 2 sweet potatoes (bio is preferable)
- 2 eggs
- 2 tbsp green onion for garnish
- Salt and pepper to taste

Method:

1. Clean the sweet potatoes (do an extra good job if you are going to keep the skins on for extra nourishment).

2. Chop sweet potatoes into bite size pieces. In a skillet, heat 2 tbsp olive oil over medium-high heat and roast the potatoes -- stirring them occasionally.

3. Chop the ends off of zucchini and send them through the spiralizer.

Method (Avocado Spread):

1. Combine your avocado and garlic together with 2 tbsp olive oil and water in a blender/ food processor. Use your best judgment: you may need to add a tad more olive oil to produce the full, creamy outcome you are aiming for.

2. Drizzle the avocado cream over your zucchini noodles.

3. Potatoes are added when they are fully cooked and slightly browned.

4. Add two cook two eggs (any way you like them...this means hard boiled, soft boiled, poached, over easy etc..) **For hard boiled eggs, add eggs to boiling water just after your potatoes have begun cooking.

5. Garnish your beautiful island of green with onion, salt and pepper and by all means, enjoy!

Song of Salorville

Song of Saylorville draws from staple foods often grown in the midwestern region of the United States that is often referred to as the "Breadbasket." This is also a major pork producing region. During long, hot summer days in Iowa droves of farmers spend their afternoons at Saylorville Lake. It is an idyllic spot for fishing, boating and barbecuing.

Because of Iowa's sweltering heat, pork is not considered an appealing afternoon dish. Song of Saylorville was invented as a creative way to use otherwise unwanted pork during those sizzling summer months. It is not only tasty and packed with nourishment, it combines indredients that enable the body to function well during spells of warm weather.

Pork packs a punch, too. It is rich in B12, B6, Thiamin (B1), Niacin (B3). What happens when you get all those B vitamins together? They convert food into fuel that gives the body a nice energy pick-me-up. Thiamine aids many body functions including the nervous system, muscle function, and helping out electrolytes by enabling them to transport themselves in and out of nerve cells, muscle cells , as well as digestion and carbohydrate metabolism. Eggs adds balance to this salad, nourishing it with equal parts protein, fat and carbs. Eggs also act as a source of vitamins A and C and iron. Avocados are bursting with vitamin K as well as B6, C, and E. They are a rich source of potassium and magnesium. There are over 20 minerals and vitamins in these tropical gems, so instead of listing them all we are just going to remind you, avocados are good to eat!

Ingredients:

- ¼ pound pork breakfast sausage or bacon
- 2 eggs, hard-boiled
- 3 cups cherry tomatoes, halved
- ¼ cup purple onion, chopped
- 2 avocados, diced
- ½ cup fresh cilantro, chopped
- ½ teaspoon kosher salt
- ¼ teaspoon black pepper
- 1 lemons, juiced

Method:

1. Roll the sausage into 1-1/2 inch meatballs. Over high heat, cook and stir until brown on all sides and cooked through. Set aside to drain and cool.
2. Peel the eggs and cut each into 8 pieces.
3. Combine the eggs, tomatoes, onion, avocado, meatballs, cilantro, salt, pepper, and lemon juice into a large mixing bowl.
4. Stir until the egg yolks and avocado becomes a little creamy.
5. Now, you are ready to serve your dish!

Thursday's Salad

Sometimes (probably often) while dieting the best option is to uncover what you can make that will quench your thirst for tastes that are familiar. Thursday's Salad is just that. It is a simple green salad topped with a Ranch Dressing that aligns itself with the Whole30 rules.

Ingredients (salad):

- 1 bag of leafy green lettuce (this can be a lettuce mix, spinach, romaine lettuce, or even iceberg lettuce)
- 4 carrots
- 1 beef tomato

Method:

1. Clean lettuce, dry and put in a deep salad bowl.
2. Peel carrots, chop and (add to bowl).
3. Clean and dice tomato (add to bowl).

A Home on the Range Dressing

Ingredients (dressing):

- ⅔ light olive oil
- 1 egg
- 2 teaspoons red wine vinegar
- ½ teaspoon sea salt
- ½ teaspoon black pepper
- 1/2 teaspoon onion powder
- 1 tablespoon dried herbs or handful chopped fresh dill
- 2 tablespoon full-fat canned coconut milk/ coconut cream**

To assure it is whole30, use coconut milk with no sulfites

Method:

1. Combine your egg, red wine vinegar, spices and herbs in a blender or food processor. Be mindful not to not over blend.
2. Delicately, pour your olive oil into the top of food processor/blender while running it on slow speed.
3. Now, add the coconut milk and pulse a few more times and voila!

Chapter 9: Whole Food Slow Cooker Challenge Dessert Recipes

It is often said the Whole30 Diet dessert does not exist. We do not agree. Here we have compiled various sensational dessert recipes for you. We believe each of them can be easily tweaked as any ingredient is easily interchangeable with your fruit preference. This is a chance for you to get really creative and groove to your own tune, if you wish.

Long Hot Summer

The South loves food and we love the South. There is no denying Georgia is one of our favorite resources when it comes to discovering new recipes. Small towns like Bainbridge, Georgia offer up some of the most tempting dishes, almost all of them are inspired entirely by locally grown products. Long Hot Summer demonstrates peaches even in their most simple form can be a delicacy. In the summer's folks head to Bainbridge to celebrate River Town Days where one of the most popular desserts is a simple cold plate of peaches topped with cinnamon and almonds.

Peaches are a source of fiber and vitamin C. Almost aid in digestion and other bodily functions.

Ingredients:

- 4 ripe peaches
- 1 ½ tablespoons extra virgin olive oil
- ¼ cup slivered almonds
- 1 teaspoon vanilla essence
- 1 tablespoon ground cinnamon

Method:

1. Cut peaches in half, remove stones and cut the flesh into thick wedges.
2. Add peach wedges cut side down and cook for 2-3 minutes, tossing frequently.
3. After the heat has bleed sweetness from peaches, place the peaches in the refrigerator, cut side upward facing.

4. 10 minutes before serving remove peaches from refrigerator, add them to their serving dish.

5. Heat 2 teaspoons of the olive oil in a frying pan over medium high heat and cook almonds for 1-2 minutes, stirring constantly, or until just golden. Remove almonds from pan and set aside.

6. Wipe out the pan with a paper towel then add remaining 1 tablespoon olive oil and vanilla essence and cinnamon.

7. Drizzle your peaches with olive oil vanilla sauce and top with almond slivers.

8. Serve!

Frisco Fried Bananas

It should come as no surprise one of our wackiest Whole30 dessert recipes originates from San Francisco where what's alternative is commonplace. This recipe emerged from within the Asian and Hispanic culinary influences that have existed in San Francisco over the past several decades. The recipe grew heavily in popularity during the 1960's when the drug culture was all the rage. The "fried" part of the recipe has a double meaning. The bananas are fried but so were most of the population who derived the most satisfaction from this dish which was a hit created by a street vendor near the Tenderloin District.

Bananas are an supreme source of potassium. Spices used here have a number of medicinal properties that aid the body in keeping it in prime working condition; they are also rich in minerals.

Ingredients:

- 2 medium, firm bananas
- ½ teaspoon ground cinnamon
- ½ teaspoon ground cloves
- ½ teaspoon ground nutmeg
- 1 cup walnuts
- 1 tablespoon extra virgin coconut oil **

***To assure it is whole30, use coconut milk with no sulfites*

Method:

1. Slice the bananas and sprinkle with cinnamon, cloves, nutmeg.
2. Heat a large skillet over medium heat, about 3 minutes.
3. Add the coconut oil and swirl to coat**.
4. Add the banana slices in a single layer.
5. Cook until golden, 2-3 minutes on each side.
6. Cover generously with walnuts.

To assure it is whole30, use coconut milk with no sulfites

Constellations

Ingredients:

- 4 apples, skins peeled, sliced (Granny Smith or Pink Lady)
- ½ tablespoon cinnamon
- ½ tablespoon nutmeg
- ½ tablespoon allspice
- ½ tablespoon cloves
- ½ tablespoon cardamom
- 1 tablespoon orange zest
- ½ tablespoon molasses
- 1 tablespoon ginger
- 1 tablespoon coconut butter**

Method:

1. In a saucepan or a cast iron skillet over medium heat, warm coconut butter.
2. Add the apple wedges, stirring them around to coat them in the coconut butter for five minutes, stir (your aim is a golden brown tone).
3. In a bowl, add your variety of spices together and blend them thoroughly, pour over your apples and stir.
4. Let the apples cook for a couple more minutes until all of the indredients have caramelized together and the apples are soft.
5. Remove apples from heat and drizzle with molasses before serving.

Tropical Island Skewers

On the mountainous island of Sicily, the well-known volcano of Mount Etna coughs up smoke constantly. During the summer months, those living under the Ionian sunshine and beside a hot bed of fresh lava make a million uses of fresh fruit which grows wildly well there. Etna's ashes are like gold. The sprinkle the fields making them mineral rich and able to grow nearly anything. Merging the climate, the fruits, and the volcanic fury, is a recipe that is exciting as it is tasty. Using different combinations of the meatiest fruits over a grill transforms into an exotic dessert that is colorful, fun and incredibly easy to make.

Ingredients:

- 1 watermelon - cut into cubes
- 1 cantaloupe - cut into cubes
- 1 pineapple - cut into cubes
- 2 peaches - cut into wedges
- balsamic vinegar
- 2 tbsp fresh basil, chopped

Method:

1. Ready your grill by letting it get hot.
2. Begin the process of slicing your fruit varieties into cubes that are as equal in size as possible.
3. Decorate your skewers with the cut up fruit.
4. Once your grill is ready, place the skewers on it. Grill for about 3-4 minutes on each side. You want the fruit to start to blacken and soften but not get too mushy. Remove from the grill once finished.
5. Drizzle balsamic vinegar, and add chopped fresh basil.

Pine-Lime Ice Capade

This is the type of recipe that serves as a perfect example of fun, easy desserts. It was created by a 12-year- old duo who tired of selling lemonade at their summer stand on the corner of Lincoln and 5th street. They now offer several versions of their ice capades and even have different offerings for children and adults.

We are using an adult version!

Ingredients:

- 3 cups ripe pineapple, roughly chopped
- ¼ cup lime juice
- Pinch of sea salt

Additional Necessities

- Popsicle molds
- Food-grade popsicle sticks

Method:

1. Combine both pineapple and lime juice along with a pinch of sea salt in a blender -- mix on high.
2. Fill your popsicle molds. Leave a little space at the top of each one -- they will expand upon freezing for 5-7 hours.

Pear and Apple Canoes

These little treats come from the Caribbean islands where coconut and pears are plentiful. With an abundance of fruit varieties, some chefs have taken to looking beyond flavors, concentrating on what objects in the world around us food can represent.

Ingredients:

- 1 large apple, peeled and sliced in half
- 1 large pear, peeled and sliced in half
- 2 tablespoons coconut oil **
- 2 tablespoon ground cinnamon
- ¼ teaspoon fine grain sea salt
- 3 tablespoon coconut butter, melted**

**To assure it is whole30, use coconut milk and coconut butter with no sulfites*

Method:

1. Warm your skillet over medium heat, add coconut oil.
2. When coconut oil is sizzling hot, add fruit halves, sliced side facing down.
3. When golden crust has formed, remove fruit halves, set aside on serving plates, sliced side facing upward.
4. In skillet melt your coconut butter, add cinnamon and salt.
5. Drizzle sauce into the pear divot and over the top of your apple halves.
6. Serve.

Chapter 10: Whole Food Slow Cooker Challenge Smoothie Recipes

Smoothies are easy to make and they are something everyone loves. It is well worth invest in a blender if you do not already have one. Many websites will list reasons why a high powered blender is a must have. However, rather than spending $600 dollars pick a run of the mill blender up a Target. Give it a go and calculate how often you actually use the device before taking the next step and upgrading.

A few tips and tricks to making smoothies!

Frozen bananas are as good as ice!. Peel, slice, and freeze them. Or if you want to, do not take the peel off. It has a lot of nutrients and while it is not as easy to chew raw, when put through a blender you can ingest it in just one unsuspecting sip. If you do decide to toss the banana in peel and all, we encourage you to buy organic bananas. The rather thick peel protects the fruit from many insecticides and does a far better job than an apple peel at this job due to the banana peels thickness. Despite this, bananas are regularly sprayed with chemicals you do not want to add to your food dish. It is easy to avoid and honestly, organic bananas are slightly smaller and sweeter -- you cannot lose.

Luscious Lucy

Ingredients:

- 1-2 ripe bananas -- start with one banana and add more if you need it to be sweeter
- 1 cups frozen mango
- ½ pitted avocado
- ½ cup frozen pineapple
- 1-2 big handfuls of baby spinach
- 2 cups water or unsweetened almond milk

Method:

1. In a blender, combine almond milk, bananas, avocado and spinach.
2. Blend until everything is well mixed.
3. Add frozen mango and frozen pineapple. Blend again until everything is smooth.
4. Pour into cup.
5. Enjoy immediately!

Pretty in Pink

Ingredients:

- 1 cup coconut milk **
- 1 tablespoon chia seeds
- 2 frozen bananas
- ¼ a large beet
- 2 cups frozen raspberries
- 1 cup almond milk

**To assure it is whole30, use coconut milk with no sulfites*

Method:

1. Preheat oven to 375 F. Wash, peel and trim your beet.
2. Cut in half and put on a small baking sheet.
3. Roast for 45-60 minutes or until fork tender.
4. Let cool completely.
5. Combine everything in a blender.
6. Add extra almond milk until desired consistency is found.

Bradley's Breakfast

Ingredients:

- 2 frozen bananas
- 2 cups coconut milk
- 2 tablespoons nutmeg
- 1 tablespoon cinnamon to taste

**To assure it is whole30, use coconut milk with no sulfites*

Method:

1. As your banana is frozen, be sure to add it in small bits to the blender.
2. Pour in coconut milk – blend.
3. Add spices.

Maui Monday

Ingredients:

- 1¼ cups of cold apple juice
- 1 ripe banana, sliced
- 1 kiwifruit, sliced
- 5 frozen strawberries

Method:

1. Add apples juice and banana – blend.
2. Add kiwi and strawberries.
3. Pour into cup -- enjoy!

Key West

Ingredients:

- 1 cup coconut milk
- 1 banana, peeled, sliced, and frozen
- 1 mango, skinned and chopped
- 5 large strawberries, halved

Method:

1. Pour coconut milk and banana into blender – blend.
2. Add remaining indredients --- blend.
3. Serve!

Sweet Virginia

Ingredients:

- 1 plum, pit removed, wedged
- 1 peach, pit removed, wedged
- 1 nectarine, pit removed, wedged
- 1 banana
- ½ cup blueberries, fresh or frozen
- 2 cups almond milk

Method:

1. Mix banana and almond milk until well blended.
2. Pour additional fruits into blender -- take care to add frozen indredients slowly and blend between switching fruits as to avoid clogging the blender.
3. Blend everything until a thick.
4. Spoon into cup. Enjoy!

Boston Dream

Ingredients:

- 1 cup almond milk
- 1 cup pumpkin puree
- 2 teaspoons cinnamon
- 1 apple, cored
- Dried cranberries (unsweetened)

Method:

1. Mix almond milk with pumpkin puree.
2. Add cinnamon, apple and cranberries.
3. Add additional almond milk depending on consistency desired.
4. Pour.
5. Enjoy!

Central Park

Ingredients:

- ¼ cup carrot juice
- ½ cup orange juice
- 1 cup spinach
- 1 cup roughly chopped kale, ribs removed
- 4 small broccoli, sliced and frozen
- 1 banana, peeled, sliced, and frozen
- 1 apple, cored and roughly chopped

Method:

1. Add carrot juice, spinach and kale – blend.
2. Add orange juice along with broccoli – blend.
3. Add banana and apple – blend.
4. When desired consistency is reached, enjoy!

Bar Harbor

Ingredients:

- 1 cup of pomegranate juice
- 2 cups of frozen blueberries
- 1 cup strawberries
- 1 cup blackberries
- 1 cup raspberries

Method:

1. Add pomegranate juice and blueberries – blend.
2. Slowly add remaining cups of berries to the mix -- blend intermittently to avoid slowing the blender's blade.
3. Pour and enjoy!

Splendor by the Door

Ingredients:

- 1 cup of grapes
- 3 kiwis, peeled
- 1 apple, peeled, seeded
- 1 pear, peeled, seeded
- 1 cup pineapple juice

Method:

1. Blend pineapple juice with grapes, kiwi, apple and pear.
2. Enjoy!

Trick or Treat?

Ingredients:

- ½ cup of almonds
- 1 cup of pitted dates
- 1 cup almond milk

Method:

1. Blend and enjoy!

Greenwich Village

Ingredients:

- 2 bananas
- 2 cup strawberries
- 1 cup almond mil

Method:

1. Add everything to your blender – blend.
2. Enjoy!

Key Largo

Ingredients:

- 1 cup coconut milk
- 1 frozen banana
- ½ avocado
- 1 tablespoon lime zest
- 1 tablespoon lime juice

Method:

1. Combine everything except the lime zest and lime juice – blend.
2. Add lime zest – blend.
3. Taste adding lime juice as desired.

Chapter 11: Slow Cooker 30 Day Challenge Menu

WEEK ONE

BREAKFAST

DAY1 SMOOTHIE
DAY2 EGGS, SWEET POTS, MEAT
DAY3 SMOOTHIE
DAY4 OMELETTE
DAY5 SMOOTHIE
DAY6 SMOOTHIE
DAY7 OMELETTE

LUNCH

DAY1 LEFTOVERS
DAY2 LEFTOVERS
DAY3 LEFTOVERS
DAY4 LEFTOVERS
DAY5 *THURSDAY'S SALAD*
DAY6 LEFTOVERS
DAY7 *LISBON BY THE SEA*

DINNER

DAY1 ORANGE ZEPHYR POACH

DAY2 MOORLAND THYME & CHICKEN

DAY3 SAN SEBASTIAN TAGINE

DAY4 SOUTH PACIFIC BLUE SONG

DAY5 SYRACUSE CHICKEN AND OLIVES

DAY6 SEVEN BRIDGES ROAD

DAY7 TURBULENT HAROLD

WEEK TWO

BREAKFAST

DAY1 SMOOTHIE

DAY2 EGGS, SWEET POTS, MEAT

DAY3 SMOOTHIE

DAY4 OMELETTE

DAY5 SMOOTHIE

DAY6 EGGS, SWEET POTS, VEGGIES

DAY7 SMOOTHIE

LUNCH

DAY1 Leftovers

DAY2 Leftovers

DAY3 Leftovers

DAY4 CORNWALL JUBILEE

DAY5 Leftovers

DAY6 Leftovers

DAY7 COCONUT GROVE

DINNER

DAY1 BOMBAY CURRY CHICKEN
DAY2 ANARCHY IN ANCHORAGE
DAY3 PARIS PATELLA
DAY4 PEPPERDINE STEAK
DAY5 LUSTROUS LUCY
DAY6 NATCHEZ WEEKEND
DAY7 KC SHORT RIBS

WEEK THREE

BREAKFAST

DAY1 SMOOTHIE
DAY2 EGGS, SWEET POTS, MEAT
DAY3 SMOOTHIE
DAY4 HARD BOILED EGG
DAY5 SMOOTHIE
DAY6 OMELETTE
DAY7 SMOOTHE

LUNCH

DAY1 PEACH AND WHITE FISH SALAD
DAY2 Leftovers
DAY3 Leftovers
DAY4 SONG OF SAYLORVILLE
DAY5 Leftovers
DAY6 Leftovers
DAY7 EASY GREEN FOREST SALAD

DINNER

DAY1 MARRAKESH EXPRESS
DAY2 THE LOVING KISS
DAY3 ADRIATIC MARRIED MEATBALLS
DAY4 CORNWALL JUBILEE
DAY5 LOUISIANA STEAM
DAY6 SARDINIA SATURDAY
DAY7 LINCOLNSHIRE LAMB

WEEK FOUR

BREAKFAST

DAY1 SMOOTHIE
DAY2 EGGS, FRIED VEGGIES
DAY3 SMOOTHIE
DAY4 OMELETTE
DAY5 SMOOTHIE
DAY6 EGGS, SWEET POTS, MEAT
DAY7 SMOOTHE

LUNCH

DAY1 Leftovers
DAY2Leftovers
DAY3 Leftovers
DAY4Leftovers
DAY5Leftovers
DAY6Leftovers
DAY7 ALVARADO ISLAND SALAD

DINNER

DAY1 NEW CASTLE LAMB CURRY

DAY2 BOMBASITY BY THE BAY

DAY3 CINNAMON CHUCK

DAY4 JOHNNY APPLESEED

DAY5 CREAMY DREAMY

DAY6 BERLIN BEER GARDEN SOUP

DAY7 WELLFLEET & VINE

Chapter 12: Whole Food Slow Cooker Challenge Grocery List

This list of a compilation of ingredients you will need to get going with your 30 Day Whole Food Slow Cooker Challenge.

MEAT/FISH

Salmon
White Fish
Shrimp
Tuna Steaks
Ground beef
Eggs
Chicken breasts
Chicken whole
Chicken Broth

PRODUCE

Oranges
Raspberries
Onion
Garlic
Carrots
Fennel
Peaches
Lime

Onion
Zucchini
Coconut Milk
Coconut Butter
Almond Milk
Sweet Potatoes
Mango
Celantro
Mixed Greens -- lettuce

EVERYTHING ELSE

Blanched almond flour
Spices**

Chapter 13: Oven to Slow Cooker Conversion

Traditional Recipe:
15 - 30 mins

Slow Cooker:
1 - 2 hours on High
4 - 6 hours on Low

Traditional Recipe:
30 mins - 1 hour

Slow Cooker:
2 - 3 hours on High
5 - 7 hours on Low

Traditional Recipe:
1 - 2 hours

Slow Cooker:
3 - 4 hours on High
6 - 8 hours on Low

Traditional Recipe:
2 - 4 hours

Slow Cooker:
4 - 6 hours on High
8 - 12 hours on Low

*****Root vegetables take longer than meat to cook. Adjust by placing them near the heat source, at the bottom of the pot.*

Conclusion

When gathering recipes for the Whole30 diet we wanted to eliminate the idea of food restrictions by finding compelling and enticing recipes to enhance your day to day experience. Our goal is to illustrate how the elimination of certain foods does not empty your table from having a wealth of exciting and delicious options. This is why we have comprised our cookbook of sample recipes from around the globe. Along with that, we were trying to address a question that continues surfacing is what a person is supposed to do once they complete a 30 Day Whole Food Slow Cooker Challenge.

We think the answer is, assess how you feel and consider what items you miss and those that you don't. Now that you have finished you might want to treat yourself to a glass of wine or a slice of bread or both! After being away from sugar and wheat, pay attention to how your body feels when reintroducing them. For some, a little sugar will taste great but might also cause you to feel a little bit tired after your body digests it. Sugar crashes are hard to detect when the normal routine includes sugar on a regular basis.

This is the same with all the items you have eliminated from your plate over the duration of your 30 Day Challenge. More than any eliminated ingredient, most doctors concur, sugar is not healthy for us. You may notice after being on the Whole30

Diet that many breads, cereals, and even the bacon you buy are packed with Corn Syrup. It is impossible to detect without going away from it for a period of time. Now that you have, see if you can taste the difference.

After Whole30 you may be compelled to eat sugar based foods, but not eat foods that sugar or corn syrup has been added unnecessarily. This is how Whole30 can be life changing. On day 31 you are reintroducing yourself to a food world with a clean palate, a clean blood stream, and a clean mind.

You have prepared yourself to become a different kind of consumer. At the same time, you have opened your kitchen to a vast array of dishes. The more knowledge you develop around food, the better able you will be to construct a diet that fits you -- and only you. There is not a one size fits all cookbook that can fulfill everyone's culinary yearnings. Nonetheless, we very much hope we succeeded in fulfilling yours.

Made in the USA
Lexington, KY
29 September 2017